*Ladies Love Yourselves First,
That's Happiness*

Ladies Love Yourselves First, That's Happiness

Cadori

All Rights Reserved. No portion of this book may be reproduced, stored in a retrieval system, or transmitted in any form or by any means-electronic, mechanical, photocopy, recording, scanning, or other-except for brief quotation in critical reviews or articles, without the prior permission of the publisher.

Published by Game Changer Publishing

ISBN 9798573529868

GC | Game Changer
PUBLISHING

www.PublishABestSellingBook.com

Dedications

I dedicate this book to my five children, Bobby aka Dougie (Rest in Heaven), Shabije', Amber, J, and Aesja. You all are the reasons that I decided to better myself and climb to a higher place in my life, spiritually, mentally and financially. It's because when I became a mother I vowed to myself, deep down within, and to God, to give my children the best that I had to give. The best advice, the best support, and the best upbringing that I knew how to give. So, even in my mistakes, I've tried to do my best to learn, grow and offer each of you my unconditional love and support. Each one of you will always be my heartbeats and I will always love you all unconditionally, the best way that I know how, with God leading the way. I pray that each of you will prosper and live your lives to the fullest and in your God-given purpose.

Love, Mom

I dedicate this book to my mama, Doris. Mama, you not only gave birth to me, but you taught me many lessons that I still value to this very day. From teaching me how to make meals from scratch when I was only 8 years old, to the importance of diligently studying in school to make good grades, to being committed to one man when you're married. Although my marriages didn't last forever like yours did, I did value my marriages when I was in them, because I believe in marriage if two people are committed to each other. So many lessons you've taught me, even lessons unspoken. Overall, I know that you did the best that you knew how to, given the young age that you were married, and the tremendous responsibility of having and raising 13 children.

I love you with all of my heart, and the lessons that you've taught me have helped to make me who I am today. You have always been a very smart person and even now your mind is intact, and your memory is on point! I want you to know that I will make you proud and I will help other women from the lessons that you have taught me. Mama, You are My First Love

I dedicate this book to my oldest brother, Fred. Big brother, where would I be today without your love, support and guidance? You helped raise me and take care of me, even when you were just a teenager. I will never forget that. And I could never repay you for that! You are the one person on this planet that knows me better than I know myself. Your words of wisdom are always with me. So much so, that each of my children can quote things that you've told me because I've shared your words with them ever since they were small children. All of my children have the utmost respect for you, and Dougie looked up to you and respected you to the max!

You are the one and only person I go to for sound advice and wisdom. Anything of importance in my life is shared with you first. All I know is that I would not be the person that I am today if it wasn't for your love and guidance throughout my entire life. I'm happy to be your sister and I hope I make you proud.

I Love You Endlessly Big Brother

DOWNLOAD YOUR FREE GIFTS

Read This First

Just to say thanks for buying and reading my book, I would like to give you a 100% bonus gift for FREE, no strings attached!

To Download Now, Visit:

www.CadoriTheAuthor.com/CM/FreeGift

Ladies Love Yourselves First, That's Happiness

Cadori

Game Changer PUBLISHING

www.PublishABestSellingBook.com

Dedication

I dedicate this book to my five children, Bobby aka Dougie (Rest in Heaven), Shabije', Amber, J, and Aesja. You all are the reasons that I decided to better myself and climb to a higher place in my life, spiritually, mentally and financially. It's because when I became a mother I vowed to myself, deep down within, and to God, to give my children the best that I had to give. The best advice, the best support, and the best upbringing that I knew how to give. So, even in my mistakes, I've tried to do my best to learn, grow and offer each of you my unconditional love and support. Each one of you will always be my heartbeats and I will always love you all unconditionally, the best way that I know how, with God leading the way. I pray that each of you will prosper and live your lives to the fullest and in your God-given purpose.

Love, Mom

I dedicate this book to my mama, Doris.

Mama, you not only gave birth to me, but you taught me many lessons that I still value to this very day. From teaching me how to make meals from scratch when I was only 8 years old, to the importance of diligently studying in school to make good grades, to being committed to one man when you're married. Although my marriages didn't last forever like yours did, I did value my marriages when I was in them, because I believe in marriage if two people are committed to each other. So many lessons you've taught me, even lessons unspoken. Overall, I know that you did the best that you knew how to, given the young age that you were married, and the tremendous responsibility of having and raising 13 children.

I love you with all of my heart, and the lessons that you've taught me have helped to make me who I am today. You have always been a very smart person and even now your mind is intact, and your memory is on point! I want you to know that I will make you proud and I will help other women from the lessons that you have taught me. Mama, You are My First Love.

I dedicate this book to my oldest brother, Fred.

Big brother, where would I be today without your love, support and guidance? You helped raise me and take care of me, even when you were just a teenager. I will never forget that. And I could never repay you for that! You are the one person on this planet that knows me better than I know myself. Your words of wisdom are always with me. So much so, that each of my children can quote things that you've told me because I've shared your words with them ever since they were small children. All of my children have the utmost respect for you, and Dougie looked up to you and respected you to the max! You are the one and only person I go to for sound advice and wisdom. Anything of importance in my life is shared with you first. All I know is that I would not be the person that I am today if it wasn't for your love and guidance throughout my entire life. I'm happy to be your sister and I hope I make you proud.

I Love You Endlessly Big Brother

Foreword

I thank God often for being born out of my mother's womb.

I cannot quantify the level of care, unconditional love and patience she has always given me. I have always felt whole in her presence, even when she was mending her own broken heart.

Very early on when I was a kid, my mom would sit me down and tell me pieces of her life story, bite-size piece by bite-size piece at a time, in hopes that I would extract the lesson she was trying to teach me — it was very clear, she wanted these lessons to propel me to a place where I wouldn't have to learn the hard way, through my own experiences. She yearned to cut my learning curve, and desperately wanted me to avoid the pain she had to face through tough life lessons, since no one took the time to sit down with her and talk about life.

I've shaped my life off of the lessons my mom taught me (and continues to teach me), along with the discipline my dad instilled. She would tell me about waiting to fall in love, finding my purpose, being grateful to God, being obedient to my parents, and being respectful, genuine and kind in my interactions with other people.

Most kids I grew up around ignored their parents advice, and many would purposely rebel against it, but there was something about the intensity, the passion and the anguish my mom faced, that I didn't want to learn anything the hard way. I listened.

I also learned through watching my mom experience pain, by overextending herself for others. We would drive ten hours to visit people, when the same care was rarely reciprocated. My mom would buy gifts for, be a listening ear to, or a shoulder to cry on, for people who didn't do the same for her when she needed them most, most notably when my eldest brother, Dougie, my mom's eldest son, was murdered. I watched her suffer through the same pain and heartbreak she told me to avoid. I watched our family fall apart at the seams, after her best efforts to keep our family together.

This seismic shift revealed every unhealed place I hadn't yet uncovered. I hadn't realized the heaviest burden I carried projected from not fully loving myself. I now had a front row seat to the best show in the world, the rise of a Phoenix from the ashes, both in my mom's life and in my own.

I watched my mom blossom into a beautiful flower. It was like watching the metamorphosis of a caterpillar into a butterfly, unveiling the truest version of herself through love and growth.

The same love I saw her give so freely to others, the same love I was raised off of, she was now able to give to herself. And just like all of the other lessons she's taught me so far in life, I watched, and I learned, and I did the same.

Through her strength I drew enough wherewithal to follow her lead, conquering depression and anxiety, loving myself to happiness and fulfillment, and my own definition of success.

This path to self love is not an easy one — working through the pain of forgiving myself, letting go of shame, and learning who I am outside of everyone's expectations of who I should be, has been the deepest work I've ever had to endure. But I roll up my sleeves with a smile on my face every morning, as I go through my gratitude list and affirmations. The beauty of self-love is worth every ounce of effort.

This book holds one of the most important keys all of us search for in life - the key to ourselves. I'm excited for you to find your truest self in these pages through my mom's life stories, just as I have from the lessons she has taught me. And who knows, someone may see you loving yourself so well they get inspired to do the same, like I did.

Thank you Mommy,

Love,

Aesja

Table of Contents

Chapter 1
Mistakes 1

Chapter 2
Childhood Trauma 11

Chapter 3
Settling for the Bottom 19

Chapter 4
Inner Circle & Accountability 25

Chapter 5
There are No Perfect People 31

Chapter 6
Red Flags 41

Chapter 7
Me-Time & Self Reflection 59

Chapter 8
Choose to be Happy & Protect Your Peace 65

Chapter 9
Distance Yourself From Negative People, Including Some Family Members 75

Chapter 10
Manifest What You Want 81

Chapter 11

Woman Warrior 87

Chapter 12

Stand in Your Power & Never Give Up 89

Bonus Chapter #1

Choose To Be Respected Rather Than Liked 101

Bonus Chapter #2

Spending Time With Yourself 105

Bonus

A Glance At What Happiness Looks Like 107

Chapter 1

Mistakes

Let us talk about failures right out the door. Once we put everything on a table and acknowledge it, only then we can extract the lessons from it and move on in life. Where we often go wrong is when we hide things from ourselves. We lie to ourselves and we tell ourselves that there is no problem. And if we have no problem, then there is no lesson to learn from because we are not acknowledging our mistakes, which hinders us from becoming a better version of ourselves.

I want to start by telling you about some mistakes that I made a long, long time ago. When I was in my twenties, I made a lot of mistakes. As a young mother and not having a lot of income led me down a path where I was not proud of the bad choices that I made. When I was in my mid-twenties, I had a job where I was barely making slightly more than minimum wage. At that time in my life, I already had two children and was married. My husband was making more than minimum wage, but still not enough for a family of four. We were merely scraping by. To get by, I started to write bad checks at grocery stores as it allowed me to go over the amount of the purchase and receive $20 to $100 cashback. It all started out just getting cash back for money from essential grocery items like food, milk, and diapers. My practice of writing bad checks came to a point where it landed me in jail. Having experienced poor living conditions behind bars, I still did not learn my lesson.

Cadori

I got locked up a few times more for writing bad checks. The last time I got locked up kept me away from my children for some months before I was bailed out - that was when I finally learned my lesson! The feeling of being away from my children for a long time nearly killed me. While I was locked up I made a decision that changed my life forever. It hit home for me and I started realizing that it wasn't worth it to spend time in jail for a few hundred dollars at best. If family members fail to pool the money up to bail you out, then you're just stuck in there. You are lucky if you get a bail hearing and they lower your bail, which was not the case for me. Your life is essentially in the hands of other people once you get locked up. People are going back and forth about why you're locked up, or whatever they want to debate about you, you're just sitting in jail wasting your life away. Now keep in mind that I have never used any drugs my entire life, and I've never killed anybody either. But when you're locked up, you're in jail with everybody who has done all types of crimes. It is no secret that many crazy sick ass people in this world are in jail. But here's the kicker, most bad people never get caught. Most killers, rapists, child molesters, and just despicable people walk free amongst us all every single day. It's true what they say, a whole lot of really bad people never get caught.

While I was in jail I started reflecting on my life and putting together a plan for my future. I thought about what landed me in jail and how I could do things differently moving forward. I began to write things down on paper. One thing about being locked up is that you have a lot of time on your hands to plan and read and get to know yourself better. I made my mind up that I needed to make more money to live the life that I wanted to live. I needed to figure out what I needed to do to make money legally. It took me back to one of my dreams when I was in high school and that was to become a nurse. Needless to say, when you have children, it's much harder to go to college and study and learn, at the same time make time for family. Nevertheless, I still wrote down a plan to first get a job once I got out and then to get into a nursing school as soon as possible.

Ladies Love Yourselves First, That's Happiness

After being incarcerated for several months, I finally got bailed out. It cost my family a hefty amount of $6000 to get me out. My husband couldn't afford to get me out by himself at that time. And my family wasn't getting the money up because they were going back and forth about the politics of why I was even in jail. They didn't like my husband either, so none of them were even trying to work together to help me get out. It was just a whole lot of family drama as I sat in jail away from my children. If nothing else, that experience taught me that I never want to be locked up and have to depend on anyone to set me free. Because you never really know how people will treat you until you are in a dire situation. I learned to make myself accountable for being locked up and that's what propelled me to my success. The lessons that I learned from writing bad checks and having to have my freedom taken away from me was a very pricey one. It shouldn't have had to come to that, but when you're in survival mode, especially if you have mouths to feed a lot of times you'll find yourself in a very bad situation financially that could land you in jail.

When I got out of jail this time, I made a plan to work for six months and then apply and get into nursing school. And that's exactly what I did. I didn't stop no matter how hard it got - nursing school was hard as hell. But I had my freedom and that was all I needed to make my life better for me and my family. By the time I got accepted into nursing school, I had just had my 5th baby. That's right, I had five children when I first sat down in the chair in my first nursing class. And I can remember what one of the instructors said on the very first day of nursing school just like it was yesterday. She said, *"Everyone stand up! Now look at the person to your right, now look at the person on your left,"* then she paused, then continued, *"Now, one of you won't be standing at graduation, but it's all up to you, so I'll see you all in class tomorrow."* And she walked out. Everyone stood in shock for a minute or so. But you know what I did? I got my backpack and I smiled inside and I told myself, *"Well that won't be me because I'm not failing shit, I'm finishing this nursing program on time and I'm not repeating shit either."* And guess what? I didn't repeat a single course, and people were failing and dropping out like flies every semester. But I made all A's and B's and only one or two C's out of the entire nursing program.

My daddy passed away the second week after I started nursing school. The instructors called me into their office and told me that they understand that I just lost my father, telling me I could start the nursing program the next semester because they knew that I would be sad and possibly lose focus and that the nursing program was very vigorous and so forth. After they finished talking they asked me what I wanted to do and I said, *"Thank you all for your kind and thoughtful words but I will stay in the nursing program this semester because I'm very focused and driven and my daddy would have wanted me to continue and he would be proud of me."*

And they said, *"Ok, that's great."*

The next day I was back in class. I graduated on time with my five children and my family members at my graduation. I could tell that my daddy was there in spirit, I could hear him say, *"I'm proud of you Cathy."* I cried tears of joy as I walked across the stage and received my degree because I knew that it was well deserved and I had put blood, sweat, and tears into getting that degree and God was with me the entire time!

Mistakes will happen in life. No one is perfect. It doesn't matter who you see on TV or how famous someone is or how popular people are. Everyone has made mistakes. Some people are still making mistakes and they're in their fifties and sixties and even older, and some are the same mistakes they were making in their twenties. Why? Because they didn't learn the lesson from that mistake. They just keep repeating it over and over again. If you don't learn the lesson and change that behavior, it's only going to get worse.

I want you to sit down and reflect at some point, write down some of the mistakes you've recently made like in the last year or so. Ask yourself what you've learned from those mistakes so that you can learn and grow and know that it's not about beating yourself up. Instead, it's a light bulb moment when you can sit in a bright room and shine the light on yourself so that you can see what you need

Ladies Love Yourselves First, That's Happiness

to work on to become a better person to become happier with your life. There's happiness in the truth.

Being a nurse has afforded me the opportunity to see people from all walks of life, all income levels, social levels, cultural and spiritual backgrounds- from homeless people to multimillionaires. I have taken care of all of them and everyone in between. I've taken care of babies. I've seen babies born and take their first breath and I've seen people take their last breath. I've looked after patients who tried to commit suicide and died and the person who tried to commit suicide and lived. I've taken care of some mothers in their twenties who had stage four cancer. I've sat beside them and helped them to write out their children's future birthday cards for each year because they were too weak to write to them all. I helped them to write those cards so that their loved ones would receive birthday and graduation cards, and even cards for their children's future wedding day. They knew that they only had a few months left to live and they wanted their children to have a card from their mother on all of their special occasions. I've taken care of people as old as 102 years old. I've made countless calls for my patients at their bedside on my personal cell phone so they could talk to their loved ones during their worst times of their lives. I've held too many hands to count while comforting them or just listening to their stories, or sometimes praying with my patients together with their families at the bedside. I cannot count the hugs that I've given to my patients and they've given to me. I've been in the homes of many millionaires and the level of care that I've given to them is the same as I've given to any of my patients in my 25 years in healthcare, 22 years as a registered nurse because each person is a human being.

Here are two separate encounters that I will share with you and what I remember about two of my patients, who were millionaires. I learned about money and some of the life lessons as they relate to our health. One older man was the former owner of the Houston Rockets basketball team. He was recovering from a fall. I took care of him one summer. He and I had several conversations about businesses and politics and just everyday news and events. He was incredibly well-read and we talked about many different books that we liked. He told me that he was born poor and that he didn't like how it felt being poor. He said that he was always the type of person who wanted more out of life. He was very driven at an early age in life. So with his mindset, he was able to recognize opportunities. Then an opportunity presented itself in the car business. He grabbed the opportunity right away to invest in antique cars. His investment paid off in no time. From there, his income went through the roof! So much so that he was able to buy an NBA team years later. Well, one day we were watching the news and we started a conversation about race relations and how people treat each other. He said something that I've heard many times before, but for some reason it was the way he said it that stuck with me, "*You know, life would be so much better if people would just treat people how they want to be treated, that's all there is to it.*"

I agreed with him and said, "*It's amazing to me how the people who treat people badly don't want anybody to do the same thing to them, it's just crazy.*" That conversation out of all the conversations we had stuck with me the most.

He also told me that when you have a lot of money that most people look at you for your money first, including your family and close friends. He also shared that he learned that the hard way after he added some of his family members to some of his bank accounts. They started lying to him about money that they were taking out of his accounts without his permission and what they were using the money for. One day he decided to take them off his accounts after losing a lot of money. He warned me and said to be careful because people will tell you lies all the time even about random things just to have a conversation with you so they can end up asking you for money or trying to trick you out of your money. I thought that was very sad because now you have to second guess what people's real intentions are every time you interact with them. After all the life lessons he shared with me, I started to pay attention to how people responded to him when they came around him - I found that what he had told me was very true. Most people who came to visit him were focused on money, including some of his family members.

The other patient that I took care of, was a wealthy older man who was a business owner and an engineer. He has his name on several buildings at his Alma Mater, which is one of the major universities in Texas. He wasn't born with a silver spoon in his mouth either. I was taking care of him because he had terminal cancer. I looked after him in his home. He would talk to me when he wasn't feeling too sick, which that particular day was one of his better days. He reflected on his life that day and shared valuable life lessons with me. He told me that he had committed lots of mistakes in his vigorous years.

He recalled after he graduated from college, his first job as an engineer did not pay enough to support his family. As a result of not making enough money, he ended up getting into oil and gas by accident. It was there that he was able to come up with his patent on some new things that he invented that made him millions over the years. He owed his success to his mistakes. He was able to learn and try different things and think out of the box. He refused to take the path other people expected him to take.

He also told me that if he could do it all over again, he would have not taken as many business trips out of the country because he lost valuable time with his children as they were growing up. He had a son and a daughter, and he said that he missed out on most of their preteen and teenage years because he was always traveling. And as he got older, he looked back and said, he didn't have to go on all of those business trips that he could have had his assistant or someone else to stand in for him most of those times. During those final weeks of his life, he did a lot of self-reflection - of which some of it he shared with me. The more he shared with me the more I began to think to myself, that in the end, money and material things mean absolutely nothing compared to the time that you can't get back and the previous memories that were lost with your family and loved ones.

Cadori

Another thing that he shared with me was that health was the most important thing in life and no amount of money can take the place of your health. He further stated that if he could do it all over again, being his current state of health, he would have given his fortune away to have his health back. That struck me very deeply because here I am taking care of this brilliant man, in his mansion, which was full of beautiful priceless things all throughout the house. Possessions that he had acquired from different countries, where he had traveled with his wife or just by himself over the years. To hear him say that *"I would give all of this back and all of my wealth to have my health back,"* was very powerful!

At that moment, I knew that most people have it all wrong! That money and material things mean absolutely nothing if you don't have your health and strength. We should all be happy and grateful to just be alive and healthy because that is priceless!

Your value is what you tell yourself about you, so stop seeking the approval from others because you don't need it.

Chapter 2

Childhood Trauma

Childhood trauma, a lot of deep pain that most of us feel is rooted from childhood. The thing about childhood trauma(s) is it's so powerful, which can affect us to our very core, yet it's barely discernible. Beyond ourselves, no one can see, experience, and erase this pain. As a child, I grew up in a large family. There were a total of 13 siblings, mother, and father in the house. Between the oldest child and the youngest child is about a 22-year age difference. My childhood trauma stemmed from verbal and physical abuse.

I am the oldest daughter out of the 13 siblings. Being the oldest girl, there was a lot of pressure and a lot of responsibility put on me at a very young age. My oldest brother Fred had a lot of responsibility and pressure put on him too as a child because he was the oldest.

I do have some fond childhood memories too. I remember when I was around 8 or 9 years old having to go in the kitchen with my mama and learn how to prepare meals from scratch to help feed the family. I loved it at the time, making cornbread from scratch, making peach cobbler, frying chicken, cutting up collard greens, cutting up sweet potatoes. I loved all of it. Even to this day, I'm one of the best cooks in our family, if I say so myself. I feel happy every time I go into the kitchen and make meals for the family. Those were some of the happiest times in my childhood. But most of my childhood wasn't as happy as I thought it could be. I think it's because I had to be a miniature mother as a child, my mama and daddy were on the go most of the time, partly because my daddy was an entrepreneur. That meant that my oldest brother Fred and I had to stay home and help raise our siblings for most of our childhood, when we should have been playing outside with other children and enjoying our childhood.

Our daddy was multi-talented. He was a genius! He would work on people's cars, taking out motors and transmissions by himself, and putting in new ones, he could rewire a car, and fix anything wrong with most cars and some trucks too! He also did installation of heating and air conditioning systems for businesses and homes. He could build a house from the ground up and do all of the inside work from flooring, to wall paneling, to plumbing, as well as installing the doors and windows! I don't think I've ever met a man more talented than my daddy. And in his leisure time, he sang in gospel groups that he put together. He did not lack any talent but his issues were being overbearing with the discipline to the point of being abusive - both verbally and physically. He was more of an authoritative figure than a compassionate daddy. He was the same way with my mama, too. Especially because they had a huge age difference which was like 21 years. In my eyes, he was more of a father figure to my mama than a husband. While my daddy could be caring and loving, though very rarely, he was mostly verbally abusive. He was very set in his ways. It's his way or the highway. Listening to any other opinion about anything other than his own was not part of his vocabulary. Daddy was the controller of the household and the primary disciplinarian.

Being child-parents, meant that my oldest brother Fred and I would take care of our siblings and change their diapers and feed them whatever we had at home to eat. Some days our parents would leave off whether daddy would be doing a job somewhere at someone's home or working at a business or if they were just out and about all day. My mama would always be with him and we would be left at home to pretty much take care of all of our siblings, sometimes as many as 8 to 10 hours in one day. That meant as children, we couldn't go outside and play and enjoy what normal kids do because we were occupied taking care of our younger siblings.

Ladies Love Yourselves First, That's Happiness

In short, there was no time for play, or even just watching tv, or relaxing as a child because we had siblings to look after. God forbid, if anyone got hurt or did something that they weren't supposed to do while our parents were gone, that would mean everyone was getting a whipping as soon as they got back home.

All I know is that without my oldest brother Fred staying home and helping to raise us, I would not be where I am today. I truly appreciate him for being a smart and caring brother because he could have been rebellious and just left us at home and went with his friends instead of staying in the house all those hours with us while our parents were gone. Instead, he took care of us the best way he knew how being a teenage boy. There are so many childhood memories of my big brother being an amazing person as a child taking care of us for all those hours that my parents would be gone, but one always stands out in my mind, and when I think about it , it makes me cry every time. It was one of the times that our parents were gone for many hours again. At this time there were eight of us kids in the house with one being a new born baby. There was always a new born baby because our parents had a child every year or two. But this particular time there were eight of us and I remember being around seven or eight years old. We were hungry and didn't have much food in the house to eat at that time. Fred scrapped up some change from around the house and he counted it out and he divided up how many cookies he could get for each of us to eat. He sent me and my brother Bay (which is a nickname that I called him) to the candy lady's house with a note that he wrote for what we needed to buy. She lived about 10 houses up the street, on the same side of the street that we lived on, and when we got back home he sat at the table and divided out the cookies amongst us. As a child you don't really think too much about the details of life. You just automatically go into survival mode. As I got older and looked back over my childhood it made me see how much of a hero my oldest brother Fred really was as a child. He actually helped save our lives by being there with us and keeping us safe and free from harm. He is my very best friend for life and there is no one who could ever stand in his shoes because he helped raise me when he was just a child himself. He didn't choose to have that type of responsibility put on him, but he never left us alone, and for that I will always honor him. He gave up his childhood to help raise us. Thank you big brother, I could never repay you, I love you endlessly.

My daddy was a very controlling person, so much so that my mama was not allowed to work. I remember that one time when she applied and got hired at a dine-in restaurant behind his back. My oldest brother and I were so happy. We were literally jumping up and down with joy because her employment meant there would be some extra money for nice clothes and shoes for us. It never occurred to us that maybe mama wanted her own money, or maybe she wanted to have something to do away from her husband and children. To us, it was all about us. When daddy found out about her job, he was furious! He stormed into that restaurant and told the manager that she wouldn't be working there anymore. She only got to work there for one day - a job she really wanted and enjoyed. Out of frustration, mama packed her things and left the job because he was right there demanding that she leave. Daddy just didn't want her to work anywhere. It had nothing to do with there being a lot of children at home. Because during the day, everyone was mostly at school, so there were no children at home to look after anyway. It had more to do with him wanting total control over everything. And that's fine if that was the arrangement that they both agreed to. But mama wanted that job.

Growing up in our household, I didn't see a mama having a say in the relationship, or even with her own identity. What mama wanted to do or would have wanted to do was not talked about in our home. I had no idea what my mama wanted when I was being raised at home. What I remember seeing was my daddy working in his businesses and enjoying his leisure activities. She would support him and go to the places that daddy wanted to go to. I never saw my mama do anything for herself. Because of those things, being as they were made it harder for me to stay on jobs when I was in my twenties. Partly because I couldn't relate to seeing women go to work. I had no working-mom figure to look up to. Mama

Ladies Love Yourselves First, That's Happiness

never worked. Our parents kept us extremely sheltered. We never visited other people or visited any other family members. I can count the times on one hand that we visited grandmom's house or my cousins, aunts and uncles houses. I remember my daddy making all of the decisions when it came to discipline and everything else in our household. My mama didn't have a voice on anything as far as I could remember. I felt like she should have had a voice, because if it's a marriage, you need to be able to speak up and speak out and be heard. But that wasn't the case with my parent's relationship. As a result, whenever we were disciplined or did something that he didn't like or didn't want us to do, or even if he was just upset, say he was having a bad day, he would yell at us and curse us out. I know my daddy cursed us out and called us every name that you can think of. That happened my entire childhood. It made my self-esteem extremely low and it made me seek approval from others outside of the household. For most of my life, I didn't feel like I was good enough. That feeling extended to my adult years - that's how dreadful my daddy treated me.

I felt most of the time, I was being cursed out or even disciplined as a child was not warranted. It was more of my daddy just being controlling and upset about other things and taking it out on us siblings. His mentality was more like you do what I say, as opposed to this doesn't make any sense, or we could just talk about this or that or just let this go in some cases. Oftentimes, whatever he was yelling and cursing about wasn't even worth it. What's worse, he never gave any explanation after the discipline or after you were cursed out other than telling you to go in your room or you go sit down somewhere. That has bothered me up until the last 15 years of my life. That's when I started getting mental health therapy to help me cope with it.

Those childhood experiences were extremely traumatic. It has taken a long time for me to acknowledge those traumas and see how that has played out in my life. When those pains are not resolved, they are surreptitiously buried deep down inside of you messing up your life without you knowing. Running away from your traumas won't get you anywhere. The only way you can free yourself from the shackles of the past is to recognize and acknowledge the pain and suffering no matter how hard it is. You carry your traumas into every aspect of your life, even if you are unaware of it - it is there holding you back to some degree. A lot of people have childhood traumas. I know this because I take care of patients. From my experience, I learned that a lot of things that people who come to the hospital to be examined for a medical reason, will tell me about personal issues outside of why they're at the hospital. And trust me when I say it always goes back to their childhood. Nine times out of ten, the issues that bother them the most can be traced back to their childhood.

My motivation for bringing childhood traumas into this book, is to give you a chance to address your childhood trauma(s). Address it in private to yourself because it is important that you make it real. If you can write it down and seek professional help, similarly to what I did, and apply the knowledge and tools that you learn, it can change your life forever. That's what propelled me to heal from my childhood trauma (s). If nothing else, me realizing that just because my daddy did certain things to me, did not make it my fault. And that part was huge for me. All of those years I carried that burden of the trauma in my mind, I was blaming myself for the abuse that was done to me, without me even knowing. It was a very heavy mental load that I had been carrying all of those years. The mental health therapist taught me that everyone is accountable for their own actions. That is to say, how a person treats you has nothing to do with you but has everything to do with them and their unhealed traumas that they never got help for.

Putting that knowledge into perspective in my life meant that when my daddy would curse me out or hurt me physically, it was his fault for doing wrong and not mine. It was because he had his own unresolved traumas and that had nothing to do with me at all. I learned that the family cycles of abuse can be stopped and that I can live my life to the fullest and be happier than I've ever been without letting someone else's mistakes continue to rob me of my happiness. So I want you to sit down privately, acknowledge your childhood trauma, no matter how painful it could be, and seek professional help. Because it is the first step towards healing. You cannot change the past, it's already done, but what you can do is change how it's affecting you. From here on, cast your traumas out and not let them have power over your life anymore. Close the door on that childhood trauma. Write your own rules going forward so that you can live your life to the fullest and be happier than you've ever been before. It's in your hands now. As a result of my healing I have been able to forgive my mama for some things that I felt she could have made better in my childhood and in my young adult life. But I came to the understanding on my own that mama was a victim too. And she did the best that she could at the time being married to a controlling husband who she probably viewed as a father figure subconsciously. I let the anger go and started building the best relationship that I can with mama while she is still alive and in her right mind. I have nothing but love for my mama because she gave birth to me and she taught me invaluable lessons about life. I could never repay my mama for the love that she did give me. Her name is part of my business name because I honor her!

And to my dear mama, Doris Marshall, who is alive and well, I got you and I'll take it from here. I promise to make you proud by helping and empowering other women.

I Love You Endlessly Mama.

*Walk in your own truth and don't be afraid
to walk alone.*

Chapter 3

Settling for the Bottom

Becoming comfortable through settling for the bottom is common for a lot of people. I was no exemption, because I had adapted to that mindset many years ago. Thank goodness I was able to realize that it was not the type of life that I wanted to live for myself or for my children. One day, I just stopped dead in my tracks and made a solid plan, and began taking the steps to crawl out of the hole that I was in. I understood that to change some generational behaviors would require a lot of sacrifices. I have a little story to tell you about a childhood friend of mine, who to this very day has not fulfilled any of the dreams that she talked to me about since our childhood. She has essentially settled for the bottom. Because she has gotten comfortable living with less than she deserves.

I met her in elementary school and to this very day, we still have a cordial relationship - thanks to social media. But I remember way back in elementary school she told me that one of her dreams was to become a teacher. She was very smart throughout school until she graduated from high school. Her second choice was to be a chef. Those were the two careers that she talked about from childhood all the way through to this very day whenever we see each other. Every time I go back home to visit and I see her, she would bring up those two careers and she would ask me if I remember that those were her dreams - to which I always answer, *"Yes."*

Cadori

She ended up working at a local cleaning service cleaning office buildings for the past 20 years. She got promoted as a supervisor of a department, but at the expense of her not being disciplined enough to go through with either of the two careers that she said she's passionate about. She has settled for way less money. And as a result of that lower-income, she has not been able to live her life as fully as she would like. Oftentimes, I hear her complain about not being able to afford to travel to nice places, not being able to afford a decent car, and not being able to eat out at fancy restaurants like some of her friends do. She makes it a point to mention all of the nice places that our friends travel to from their social media posts. It was heartbreaking to hear her say that she felt bad that she was never able to even take her children on vacation when they were growing up. She also said that they have never traveled outside of their home state. Now, her children are adults and living their own lives. They missed the opportunity to travel because, according to her, she didn't have enough money. The lack of money is because she has been too afraid to go outside of her comfort zone. That way of thinking is now passed on to her children. And if they have children, they'll pass it on to them. This is how the cycles continue in families. We have to break these cycles, which oftentimes are generational curses that keep us in bondage mentally and we develop a "lack of winning" mindset. That translates to setting limitations on our ability to be our best, and push ourselves to perform better in life.

As I think about some of her complaints back down through the years, I kept reminding her that we are still alive, which means that we can still plan and save up some money to take some of those trips that she always wanted to take. I even offered to help her pay for a large portion of a trip, but she refused it. She is too afraid to branch out and do different things. Because by now I'm sure she has some extra money because she no longer has children living with her to take care of. So I asked her this question, *"When will you start living your life to the fullest and stop making excuses for the things that you want and don't have?"*

Ladies Love Yourselves First, That's Happiness

Her response was, *"Well, I'm doing my best right now, but you know I'll think of a plan later."* Which in short means, she's making another excuse, because that's the same answer she has been giving for over 30 years now.

There's a difference between living your life with a purpose and on the purpose or merely existing. Every day when you wake up, you're breathing, and you're alive! You're thankful to be alive, but what is your purpose? What are your goals and dreams and aspirations? And I've had several conversations with her through the years. A lot of it boils down to fear and what she speaks out of her mouth. *"I know I could be doing better but..."* She always has a "but" in the explanation. That word *"but,"* is an excuse. I told her that vacations can be inexpensive, which a lot of them are. If you plan for them you can start saving a little bit of money here and there, the trip will be paid for before you know it. I've sat down with her and tried to come up with a plan for her vacation trip. I know you make this salary, but let's take out a sheet of paper and write down some things that you can do. For instance, there's a trip over here. Let's say $1,000 for 5- day vacation. That includes your airfare and it includes your hotel as well. All you need is pocket money for souvenirs and food. We sat down and wrote out a plan for the $1,000 vacation. I asked her, *"How much can you realistically afford to put towards this vacation every month so, in a year or less, you can take a vacation cruise?"*

She responded right away with a tone of negativity. *"Well, I can't do this because of that and I can't do that because of this."*

Well, let's talk about what you can do. Can you work more hours on your job?

"No. Because I'm on salary."

"Okay. Can you pick up a second job and maybe work during the weekends?"

"Well, no, because I'm too tired after working this job."

Cadori

There has to be some sacrifices made! If there are things that you want in life, you have to be willing to make a sacrifice.

Sacrifice is inevitable, it works like a double-edged sword. Right now you are making a sacrifice to be on the bottom. When you're sitting on the bottom, you're not living the life you want to live. You're sacrificing your happiness because you know that deep down inside, you could be doing better. If you are willing to do things differently in your life, you'll be rewarded by more than just a trip. If you don't make enough money for the trip, pick up a second job. Even if you only work a couple of extra days a month, that could fill in the extra money that you didn't have. Then you take that money and put it into an account or in a jar to save up. And that can be your vacation money. If you work an extra two or three days a month, you've got more money to save and experience your dream vacation sooner. It's all a game of mindset after all.

If you don't want to work an extra job, start selling things on the side, like cosmetics, or candies, or anything that you know that people use very often. There are tons of things you can sell for extra income and many people do this all the time. Some call it a side hustle. The main point that I am making is that you have to have a plan. If you don't have a plan, you're going to continue to stay on the bottom and keep living the same cycle that you have been wanting to renounce.

An important fact to remember about being on the bottom is that there is nowhere else to go but up. In my friend's case, her bottom is her income. Because she has capped off with that particular job. She's on a salary and there is no significant increase for her at that company, unless she furthers her education by returning to college and getting a degree. She can't advance any further there. So, she has to decide other means to increase her income to change those things in her life that she wants. But what's for certain is this: If you keep doing the same thing, you will keep getting the same results. The settling for the bottom type of mindset is rooted in fear. And if you operate out of fear, you'll never go anywhere. So, you have to acknowledge what that fear is for you. You have to be honest

Ladies Love Yourselves First, That's Happiness

with yourself on your journey on the road to happiness. We have to fulfill our own happiness. No one else can come in and fulfill that for you. This is another step on that journey to happiness is to stop operating out of fear. I'm a big mental health advocate. Fear is something that you can get help with through mental health therapy.

Where does that fear come from? It is something that you learned because we don't come into the world being fearful of everything. Fear puts limits on your life. *"I'm not good enough,"* "Happiness is for someone else," "A new home is for someone else," "A new car is for someone else," "I can't have that purse." All of these doubts and many more are rooted in fear. Remember, you only live once. So if you want to enjoy your life to the fullest, then ask yourself when will you do it? Because once you're gone that's it for your life here on earth. You can't afford to continue to settle for less in this life. You can always choose to do everything you can do to live the life that you truly want for yourself and be happy.

Now, I want you to write down three things that you have settled for in your life that you want to change. Gather your thoughts and make a plan that will change them. If you feel you are not committed enough to make those changes, schedule an appointment with a mental health therapist to help you figure out what's blocking you from achieving your happiness. If you can write it on paper, then it can be achieved. It may take a lot of hard work or a total transformation in your life but it can be done. Believe it and achieve it!

Be clear about your goals.
Write them down, make a plan and work on them everyday.
What you believe in and work on will happen.

Chapter 4

Inner Circle & Accountability

Your inner circle and your accountability are basically a hand in hand deal. In my opinion, the people we choose to have the closest to us will definitely impact the level of success that we have. We have to choose wisely. That inner circle is very critical. It's like you're on life support. The reason why the inner circle is very critical is that this life has its challenges all alone without anyone else saying negative things to you on a daily basis or doing things to hurt you.

If you have people who are in your inner circle and they are negative, or they are toxic, you will not be able to have true happiness. Because as soon as you come up with ideas and goals to move forward, if the people around you have a negative mindset, they will discourage you because they are not happy themselves. And when people are not happy with themselves, they will not allow you to be happy.

I took care of a patient years ago, and I will never forget this person. It was a young man who was 26 years old. There were a couple of his childhood friends whom he had known since grade school, visiting him at his bedside. One of them even went to the same college as him. They were all extremely close and very influential in each other's lives. They would be considered his inner circle of friends. They did everything together. During their high school years, they started experimenting with alcohol and drugs together. They all shared lots of fun, adventurous memories. No one would ever think that the reason why he was in the hospital now was that he had attempted suicide. He came around after we were able to flush his stomach with activated charcoal to help dissolve most of the pills that he had taken. Over the next couple of days, when I was taking care of him, he started telling me about his personal life, I told him that his life was very valuable and that there are people who care about him. I inquired as to what happened to make him want to take his life. He told me that he was pretty successful in his job and was making a very nice six-figure salary. He was not in a romantic relationship with anyone at the time. He had recently moved out of his parents' house and moved to his own condo. In his newfound place, he would hang out with his two childhood friends several times every week after work. There had been another childhood friend in the group up until three months prior. Three of those four friends had a college degree and were doing pretty well for themselves financially. Only one of them in the group did not attend college, and had still been living in a home with his mom. He told me that the friend who barely made it out of high school could have been a professional football player, but he started using drugs in high school and never stopped using drugs since then. To satisfy his drug addiction, he went from using drugs to selling drugs. And his life just spiraled out of control from that point on. They would all still experiment with new drugs from time to time. What had happened to make him want to commit suicide is that one of his friends out of their group of four had recently experimented with a new drug, with them three months prior and he accidentally overdosed and died. My patient felt responsible for his friend's death. For he was the one who called him that night and told him about the new drug that their drug-dealing friend had. He was the one who drove to his apartment and picked him up and took him to meet up with their other two friends. According to my patient, his friend didn't feel like going out that night because he had to wake up early that next morning to take his father to the outpatient surgery for a procedure. He told me that his life has not been the same since that night. He barely made it through his friend's funeral and that he had not been able to talk to his friend's

Ladies Love Yourselves First, That's Happiness

parents or look them in their eyes. My patient shared his struggles with me that he can't sleep at night and he has lost his appetite - which resulted in 30-lbs weight loss just within the span of three months. He exclaimed, he doesn't want to live anymore. I merely listened to him talk for about 30 minutes then I had to leave his room to go and take care of my other patients. It was an unfortunate situation, and it was sad. I felt bad for him because his friend's overdose was accidental but he couldn't seem to get past his guilt. My patient ended up getting accepted to an inpatient psychiatric hospital. I called to check on him about a week after he left our facility and the nurse told me that he was making some progress. I checked back on him about two weeks later and he had been discharged home to continue with outpatient psychiatric therapy.

Fast forward a month later, this same patient was back in our emergency room for attempted suicide again. The ambulance brought him in after a neighbor knocked on his door repeatedly after the patient had gotten home from work but he didn't answer the door, which the neighbor said was unusual for him because he would come over and drink beer with the patient almost every evening after they got off work. So the neighbor called the police department to come and do a welfare check and good thing he did because the patient was found laying on his bedroom floor with an empty medication bottle of Valium on the floor right next to him. By the time the police arrived by breaking into the apartment, the patient was barely breathing. The ambulance was called and they had to intubate the patient immediately. My shift was near the end when the patient arrived in our emergency room. I noticed the patient immediately because he had a very distinctive red hair color and haircut.

The next morning when I arrived at work the patient had been transferred to our ICU unit and he was still on the ventilator. Two hours into my shift, I heard those dreadful words that you don't want to hear over the hospital intercom, "Code Blue ICU bed 4," which means the person's heart had stopped beating. And ICU bed 4 was the room that the patient with the distinctive red had was in, the same patient who I took care of a month before who had attempted suicide because he couldn't live with the guilt of his childhood friend accidentally overdosing on a new drug that he helped influence him to take. I was later told that they ran the code on him for almost 45 minutes trying to save him but they couldn't get him back. He was pronounced dead at 9:52 am that morning.

I took a long break after I heard about him passing away that morning. I just sat outside the hospital on a bench and I thought back to our conversation just a little over a month ago. It was very sad just thinking about how it had come to this. How two childhood friends had both died within a few months of each other and how drugs had ended both of their lives, and how the power of the influence of other people can literally cost you your life!

This was a circle of four friends, one of them wasn't really doing anything productive in his life. The other three were living independently and financially well. And they were allowing the friend who was the least productive, and who had no job, and who was hooked on drugs, and who still lived at home with his mama, to have the most influence in the group. Now one friend has used the drug that he gave him and ended up accidentally overdosing and dying. Then as a direct result of that overdose the second friend has now committed suicide because of his extreme guilt. That second friend was not responsible for his friend's accidental overdose but he convinced himself that he was. This is crucial because when we don't choose wisely, it could actually end up costing us our lives. Never mind the fact that you're not going to be able to reach your goals and dreams and enjoy any success peacefully, even if you do reach your goals, because those unsuccessful, unfocused, non-driven, goal-less people are going to constantly pull you down because they're not going anywhere. You're not going to be able to go anywhere either if you're listening to them, and they're in your inner circle.

So, who are the people in your inner circle?

Sit down, and think about it. Write down each person's name. Each person needs to be evaluated separately, and honestly. We have to first take accountability ourselves for the people who we have in our inner circle. Then we have to hold each person accountable for their actions and what they're bringing or not bringing to the relationship. So, when you make your list, each individual person's action should be evaluated. Essentially, are they adding value to your life or are they taking it away? And you have to be honest about it. If they're not adding value to your life, then that's not the person that you need in your inner circle. And the same thing is true for you as well. You should also be adding value to the people who are closest to you. It's a mutual relationship.

There's truth to the saying, *"Show me the five closest people to you, and I'll show you a picture of yourself."* Because if you're very successful and you're doing all these great things, but you have one or two people that aren't doing anything positive with their lives, just like the friend who was selling and using drugs, they can have a powerful influence over you and bring you down to their level. You're never really going to get where you're supposed to be because they're not going to allow it. If they are around you, and they're in your inner circle, there's only so far you're going to go with those people. They have weight, and their weight is going to be a heavy weight that you can't continue to carry.

So, when you look at relationship accountability in your inner circle, everyone has to be able to bring their own positivity. That positivity is their light in the relationship. No one can turn the light on for anybody else. Each person has to have it. So that light needs to shine in each person. And if they're not adding value to your life, then they're taking it away. Relationships should be a give and take, and there should not be any excuses made for anyone's actions when you're looking at accountability. So, choose wisely with your inner circle because honestly, your life could be dependent on it.

Life is so precious!
Appreciate life!
Cherish life!
Never take life for granted!

Chapter 5

There are No Perfect People

There are no perfect people. I know that may sound cliche, but to be honest, there was a time in my life, where I thought that certain people did not make any mistakes. And I know that other people can relate to this type of thinking. For example, when you think of your Pastor or religious leader, you wouldn't automatically think that these people are like the rest of us. We hold them to a higher standard and oftentimes we think of them as a symbol of perfection. In addition, to them, we may have other people in our lives that we feel are perfect as well. Let's talk about this way of thinking and come to the understanding that it doesn't matter who it is, no one is perfect. Everyone has made mistakes, and I mean everyone! There are some Religious leaders who continue lying everyday about all sorts of things. There are some politicians who lie and manipulate people all the time. There are some everyday working people who are very deceptive as well. The story I want to tell you is about a Pastor who I knew personally. He had a huge congregation. I'm talking about thousands of church members both in-person and online.

This particular Pastor (Pastor Johnson) was very judgmental. In addition to reading the Bible to you on Sunday and giving his opinion of what each chapter or each verse meant, he would go a step further and be very critical of people. You know when they're preaching on Sunday and you hear a story and somebody in the church can relate to it. Well they can relate to the sermon that he was preaching because he was actually talking about someone in the church. It would be the story of a church member who had previously come to Pastor Johnson in confidence for spiritual guidance, or to get help with an issue. Little did they know, their issues would become a Sunday sermon, which should have never been mentioned beyond their meeting. I hear this is happening a lot more now with some of these religious leaders, but it's really a breach of confidence.

When they're listening to someone's personal problems in confidence to pray for them, or to give them some spiritual guidance and they make it a Sunday sermon, that's just wrong! Pastor Johnson was very judgmental of people and he was not respectful of their private information.

So one day a huge story broke about Pastor Johnson and it was spreading like wildfire through the church. We all found out that Pastor Johnson and his wife had been having marital problems and that they had actually been separated for several months! This was a total shock to everyone in the church! Pastor Johnson had never made this known, and neither did his wife. In fact, he lied at one of the recent Sunday services and said that she had been very sick and that's why she hadn't been coming to church for the past two months. We even did a special prayer for her during that Sunday service. Everyone thought that she was dealing with a very serious medical condition.

So here we are saying a special prayer for her, only to find out that she wasn't even living with him! She had moved out! For nearly six weeks or so, no one has seen her in church. And now the cat is out of the bag and the reason is because they were separated! Not to say that he should have told us about his marital problems, but he should not have had the church praying for her for a "serious illness" that she supposedly had. And here he is representing himself as a Pastor and a righteous man, but he's just a liar who is sitting in the church pulpit!

Ladies Love Yourselves First, That's Happiness

What we later found out just blew our minds! We found out that the reason Mrs. Johnson separated from him was because she found out that he was having a love affair in the church with another woman! And that other woman happened to be the wife of one of his Deacons. She was Deacon Holmes' wife. Pastor Johnson and Deacon Holmes had been close friends since high school. The love affair had been going on for over a year. And a lot of their sexual meet ups were actually in Pastor Johnson's office at the church where he had a sleeper sofa for his late night preparation for Sunday service or a big church event. He would say that he couldn't properly focus at home so for those nights he would sleep at the church in his office. We found out through one of Mrs. Johnson's mutual friends that Mrs. Johnson learned about the love affair through his email account, after she figured out his password. Apparently he had been primarily communicating with Deacon Holmes' wife via email. And not only that, but they had been on two weekend getaways together over the past year and the hotel and flight information was also in his email account. Both weekend getaways were supposed to be church retreats that members of an out of state church invited guest Pastors to be a part of.

Well come to find out, Pastor Johnson never attended either of those retreats, but instead went to a spa hotel in Arizona both times with Deacon Holmes' wife. And Deacon Holmes' wife was supposed to be visiting her sickly, elderly parents in Rancho Cucamonga, California. So she would fly to her parents house and then call her husband to let him know that she made it there safely. Then she would let him speak to both of her parents very briefly. Her parents didn't like him and he didn't like them either. Their 20 year marriage had only caused them to like each other even less than they did from day one. And they lived in different states which were thousands of miles away from each other so they rarely visited each other and they only called each other on their birthdays. Deacon Holmes' wife knew that her husband would never call her parents because he had never called them in 20 years for anything at all. So once Deacon Holmes' wife checked in with him, she would eat lunch with her parents, then she would take another flight to Phoenix, Arizona to meet her lover, Pastor Johnson. Mrs Johnson researched and found out about all of this!

Another bombshell was discovered by Mrs Johnson while she was doing her private investigation on her rotten ass husband! After she got into the church financial records, she found out that not only was her lying ass, cheating ass husband sleeping with Deacon Holmes' wife, but that he was also having a second affair with a younger woman who was also a member of their church. Her name was Batia, a 21 year old senior in college. She was the daughter of his church accountant, Rick, who was another one of his closest friends since middle school. Pastor Johnson had recently started talking to Batia and giving her money to pay for her education. His wife found out about this affair with Batia through his text messages. The college student had been sending him nude pictures of her breasts and ass, and Pastor Johnson had been sending Batia dick pictures of himself. But to top all of that, guess what really drove Pastor Johnson's wife to move out of the house with him after being married for over twenty years? She found out that both of the women were pregnant by Pastor Johnson! Yep, Deacon Holmes' wife was pregnant by him, and the Deacon knew it wasn't his baby because he had a vasectomy six years ago and he and his wife rarely had sex.

And the college student, Batia, hadn't slept with anyone else in over nine months, so this was Pastor Johnson's baby too!

Once all that news hit the community, it was the talk of the town! Everyone was gossiping and trying to figure out how the hell did this perfect man of God live all of these multiple lives and stand in front of the congregation every Sunday and put on an act! Some church members blamed themselves for not being able to figure out what Pastor Johnson was up to, even though no one had a crystal ball, nor can anyone read anyone else's mind, they still felt some guilt, which is natural to feel when you are in shock. And this horrible information about Pastor Johnson, was very shocking.

Ladies Love Yourselves First, That's Happiness

The other half of the church members were mad as hell with Pastor Johnson! They cursed his name and vowed to never step foot into his church ever again! And some members were angry enough to want to cause him bodily harm! Everyone's emotions were all over the place! I mostly felt sadness for Mrs Johnson. My heart hurt for her and their children.

So, the church pretty much split in half. Half of the members who found out about it left the church immediately and never returned. Most of those church members had been with him for over 10 years. They just left. They no longer had any respect for him. The other half of the church members stayed and wanted to pray for the pastor and wish him well, and hope that things turned out good for him, and that he could salvage his marriage with his wife and his children. Their children were in high school at the time. It was very unfortunate, but their children had to deal with all of the backlash from their dad's infidelity, while they were in school, from the other students. It was a very hard time for them, so much so that their mom had to withdraw them from school and sign them up for a home school program. It wasn't their fault that their dad was out there sneaking around and cheating behind their families back. But they had to take the brunt of it, because he was viewed as a pillar of excellence and truth in their community. So, when something like this happens, it deeply hurts a lot of people, because they had put their trust in the Pastor.

A legal investigation was also started after his wife discovered the church bank account that had been opened to fund his mistress' wants, and the fun things that they did together. He had purchased things for them like, designer handbags and shoes, perfume, jewelry, weekend trips, hotel fees, lingerie, makeup, hair products and much more. Several former church members were threatening lawsuits against him as well. So, he had to beef up security around the church from time to time. His wife filed for divorce three months after she separated from him. And the divorce was finalized three months after she filed, which was around the time that both of his mistresses gave birth to their babies, within two weeks of each other - They both had baby boys.

The very next Sunday service, after Pastor Johnson's two sons were born, all hell broke out during that service. The Pastor was preaching, and in walks his close childhood friend, Deacon Holmes. Deacon Holmes' wife had just given birth to a baby boy that wasn't his, and he knew it wasn't his because he had that vasectomy surgery which prevented him from getting anyone pregnant. But to validate his truth he went ahead and took a paternity test, which indeed proved that the baby boy wasn't his child. So Deacon Holmes walked right down the aisle in the middle of the church and he reached the pulpit where Pastor Johnson was standing and he yelled out, *"YOU ARE THE DEVIL AND YOU NEED TO BE TAKEN OUT RIGHT NOW!"* Then he pulled out two guns and he shot Pastor Johnson 13 times, until he fell to the floor. He then turned one of the guns on himself and shot himself. All you could hear was very loud screaming and crying, and the sounds of people's feet running as fast as they could to get out of that church! Blood was all over the place and even on some of the members who had been seated on the front row, and those who were near the pulpit.

Surprisingly both men lived. The Pastor ended up in a nursing home for the rest of his life because his spinal cord was severed and he couldn't walk. He had a feeding tube and he had a tracheostomy. He was, what we in the medical field would call, a, "Total care patient." This means someone who requires 24-hour nursing care because they can't take care of themselves. Deacon Holmes ended up with a damaged colon from the self inflicted gunshot to his abdomen, and he had to wear a colostomy bag, which collects stool, for the rest of his life, but was otherwise in good health. He did have to serve one year in prison for gun violence, but he got a very mild sentence in most people's opinion, because the state that they lived in had a "crime of passion" defense. Meaning that if you hurt someone or kill someone and it was proven to be a crime of passion, then you could actually get no jail time at all.

Deacon Holmes' wife, who is now his ex-wife, filed for, and was granted a divorce. She ended up with a traumatic brain injury after a car accident. She was speeding on the highway on a rainy day

Ladies Love Yourselves First, That's Happiness

shortly after her husband was sentenced to prison for one year. She was filled with guilt about the entire love affair that she had with Pastor Johnson that had caused so many people so much pain and she wanted to end her life. So she ran her car off the road going 90 mph and she hit a tree. She didn't die but ended up with a traumatic brain injury. She has to be fed through a feeding tube for the rest of her life. Her speech is slurred and the left side of her body is weak, so she has to walk with a cane. She requires help with taking a bath and getting dressed everyday. She hired a live-in nurse aide to help take care of her toddler son. She is considered a disabled person now.

The college student, Batia, graduated and got a six-figure job. She gave her baby up for adoption. A year after she gave birth to her son she was gang raped while walking alone to her car at 3 a.m. after leaving a club. Three men raped her and she acquired HIV from that rape. She now lives with HIV, and has to take 10 different pills everyday to manage the symptoms.

The former Mrs Johnson stayed single for two years after her divorce and just focused on taking care of herself mentally and physically. She runs two miles a day, meditates everyday, and still talks to her mental health therapist once a month. She recently moved to the midwest and bought a new townhome. She opened a small clothing boutique, and she met a business owner who is a widower, and they just got engaged.

I know that this particular story may be somewhat shocking to some people, but it's real. Here we have someone who presented himself as a Pastor, who is looked at as a pillar of truth in the community, respected with the highest regards. But turns out, this Pastor was no more than the average person who makes mistakes all the time. In fact, his character was probably worse than the average person because he was knowingly deceiving thousands of people on a weekly basis by lying to them about who he really was.

I would like to ask you to start a new way of thinking today. Stop telling yourself that there are some people who are perfect, because they are not. They have problems and challenges just like all of us. We all have had ups and downs in our lives, and we will continue to have them from time to time because that's life. But when we make choices and decisions and do what's right, is when we can feel real happiness inside. It's the individual decisions that we make that show who we are. So, don't be hard on yourself. Give yourself a break and learn from your mistakes and keep moving forward knowing that everyday gives you a new chance to make your life what you want it to be. Everyday is a new day to live your life on your own terms.

Man is NOT God!
Develop your own personal relationship with God. This way you are not fooled by false profits in any form.

Chapter 6

Red Flags

I wanted to write a chapter about red flags because oftentimes we overlook them. We usually miss or ignore the red flags and proceed without any real effort on our part to call it what it is. We find ourselves dealing with a lot of stress, medical problems, different health issues such as gaining weight, overeating, undereating, and generally just unhealthy relationships. So, I would like to tell you a story about something that happened in my life — my first marriage. I was married at 18 years old, five months after I graduated from high school, and had my first baby. During the course of that one-and-a-half-year relationship, I saw a lot of red flags. I was very young and naive and in love, but those are what you call excuses when we ignore our inner voice.

I can honestly say looking back now that I wanted the relationship to work so badly, that I was willing to ignore bad things that were happening shortly after I started the relationship. I was a senior in high school. Well, it was actually during mid-junior year when the relationship first started. Even early on in the relationship, there were anger problems from my ex. There was some violence, and there were some insecurities that I saw in him. I was a child as well — a teenager — but I saw these things in this person, and I just turned a blind eye to it. Fast forward, I got pregnant, had a baby, and got married.

Of course, the marriage ended up in a divorce, which I filed for six years later. But the start of that relationship was doomed from the beginning. It wasn't just because both of us were so young at 18 years old, but because the person was doing things that just weren't healthy for any relationship. It started with telling lies, which gradually escalated to not being able to control anger when he was upset about something. It was just a lack of communication from the very beginning. My ex, who was my first husband, was a very quiet person, but when things were brought up that he didn't like or agree with, that quietness would turn into anger and then violence — punching a wall and then eventually hitting me.

I find that most women that I've come across in my lifetime would ignore the red flags. It doesn't matter the income level, race, or culture. Most women that I have friendships with or have been involved with have given these passes to men, and also other people in their lives that they have relationships with. But mostly, it is men that are given a free pass for not so good behavior. The pass is given very early on in the relationship. When we ignore these red flags, we ignore anger problems. We ignore violence. It only escalates. It's like anything else in life, really like driving a car. For example, if you get in the car and you turn the ignition on and you put it in the drive, the car is going to keep going as long as you're pressing the gas pedal. It doesn't stop until you press the brakes. If you don't press the brakes on these behaviors, these red flags are going to keep going. The red flags are not going to stop.

What I thought in my first marriage was this - If I continue to show love, make sacrifices for, and believe in this person just to stay in this marriage, they will change and they will know that I love them for sure. They will know that they're essentially good enough despite having a lot of insecurities within themselves. These insecurities, however, flowed over into our marriage. And when I decided I wanted to go to nursing school, yes, I finally decided that I wanted to go to nursing school, that person did everything they could do to deter me from going to nursing school.

Ladies Love Yourselves First, That's Happiness

As excited as I was to finally be pursuing one of my dreams since high school, that excitement was very short-lived. From day one of nursing school, my husband would start an argument about anything every time I would come home from classes. He would come home from work and before even saying hello, he would yell out, *"Every time I turn around you got that book open!"*

And I would tell him, *"It's because I'm studying, we have a test every day."*

He would then go into the kitchen and prepare dinner or whatever, but he would be fussing and mumbling the whole while saying negative words about me being in school. In fact, every time I would try to study, he would get mad. One day, after I had been in the nursing program for about two months, he finally exploded!

He came home from work and our baby daughter started crying, just as babies do. I was studying at the time. He yelled out, *"You're ignoring the baby!"*

I told him *"No, I'm getting up now to get a diaper to change her."*

Obviously, that wasn't good enough for him because the real issue wasn't even about our baby crying nor needing to have her diaper changed. It was much deeper, which I didn't realize at the time. So he kept on complaining and it escalated to the point where he yelled out *"You're just trying to go back to nursing school so you can leave me for a doctor!"*

That shocked me. I thought to myself, *"What the hell is he talking about?"* And I said to him *"What, why would I be going to nursing school to get with a doctor?"*

He was so angry, he punched a hole in one of the walls of our apartment!

I yelled back at him, *"I'm trying to get a career and a better paying job to help us!"*

43

Little did I know that in less than two months, I would no longer even be in nursing school. Little did I know that my grades would plummet so badly that I would have to withdraw midway through the short one year program to become a licensed practical nurse. Little did I know that this dream would not be coming to fruition while I was married to him. Mainly, because I couldn't peacefully study at home because he was always complaining. I couldn't even safely talk about nursing school around him because he didn't want to hear about it at all. My dream of becoming a nurse slowly diminished. I came to realize that not only was I not going to be able to complete nursing school but that I was not going to be able to attain any level of success for anything with this man. He didn't want me to become successful for fear of losing me. He had already said it out loud to me. I couldn't fully grasp the magnitude of how unequally yoked our relationship really was at that time. I was just too young and naive. All I knew was that I could not even study or talk about any of my interests and dreams to him. It was a wrap for that type of communication. But for him to not even validate my feelings about having to quit nursing school was even more hurtful to me. Once I withdrew from the nursing program and stopped going to class, he never said *"I'm sorry you had to withdraw, or maybe you can go back in the future"* or anything ever again. He sent a message to me that was loud and clear that he didn't give a damn about my dreams or my happiness.

As bad as that was, I did not realize that his behavior towards me going to nursing school was a huge red flag! It was one of the first acts that contributed to the breakdown of our marriage unbeknownst to me.

About a month later, I began to notice a change in his behavior. When he would get ready to go to work, he would iron his work clothes, which he had never done before. He had been working on this plant job, which was called the chicken house, for almost two years. I noticed that he started chewing so much gum. When I mentioned it to him, he looked shocked and said *"Oh it's because of all the smells from those dead chickens in there. It lingers in your nose and the gum helps with that."* It made sense to me but it still caught

Ladies Love Yourselves First, That's Happiness

me off guard seeing him chew the gum. I could count the times on one hand that I had seen him chew gum throughout our four-and-a-half-year relationship.

This would, in hindsight, be another red flag. I started to notice that he would put on some cologne before he would leave for work. I didn't say anything to him about the cologne at first, because I figured he would say the same thing to me that he had said about the chewing gum and the dead chicken smell. I did, however, make a mental note of it.

Later down the line, this would be yet another red flag. Frankly, the chicken house was not even a place where you would need to be wearing any type of cologne. I didn't want to start another argument with him nor have to deal with his anger issues, so I just let it go.

He had started building up this resentment towards me. The actions that he was doing against me were justifiable in his mind because of the resentment that he had against me. Soon, the answers for all of his new behavior - the ironing of clothes to wear to work, the chewing gum, the wearing cologne to work - was about to be revealed.

Now, mind you, during this new behavior stage, our sex life had also decreased as well. Truth be told, I didn't really mind that decrease because I didn't want him touching me anyway since he had been treating me badly. I'm the type of woman the moment you treat me bad, then I don't want you touching me at all!

At the time, I was working two jobs to help make ends meet. Since I was no longer in nursing school, I picked up a full-time job working four days a week to add to the part-time cashier job that I had when I was in nursing school. Both of these jobs barely paid over minimum wage.

His chicken house plant job paid him more money but still not enough for our family of four. We only had one car at the time. He would catch a ride with some co-workers from time to time, but

Cadori

for the most part, I would set my schedule and work around his work schedule so I could take him to work and or pick him up from work.

Low and behold, I drove to pick him up from work one day. Our babies were at the daycare and I had gotten off work an hour before his shift would have ended. I decided to go to his job early and just park and wait in the car. I arrived at his job about 45 minutes before he was to get off work. I parked the car and guess who I saw standing in between two tractor-trailers outside of the chicken house plant? My husband and a light-skinned woman! They were hugging and kissing! I was in total shock! I didn't know whether to get out of the car and go up to them and start fighting, or to drive off and let his ass find another way home, or to just sit there and cry. I was just frozen. I couldn't move. As the tears rolled down my face I started thinking about that goddamn chewing gum and the ironing of his work clothes and the cologne. It all hit me like a ton of bricks at that very moment! So this is why his ass has been doing all that shit, I thought to myself! I wanted to call somebody on the phone, but I couldn't think straight at the time. A million thoughts were running through my mind! *"Is this the end of our family? How could this be happening?! What did I do wrong to deserve this shit? Why is my quiet husband up here cheating on me? What am I lacking that caused this? Who else knows about this and why didn't I know that this was going on? Am I stupid or crazy? Does he hate me?"* These thoughts and many more were racing through my mind faster than the speed of light! My head was pounding! I could feel my heart racing and I felt so short of breath, I had to roll down the windows in the car to get some fresh air. Then my thoughts went to my children. *"How could he do this to our family, and what did these innocent babies do to deserve this act of infidelity to our family?"*

With all of the hurt in me and the unanswered questions going through my head, I just decided to sit there and wait for him to get off work. I was still very angry, but I wiped the tears from my eyes and I started to think about what I would do when he got in the car. I decided that I wouldn't say anything at all to him. I would just

Ladies Love Yourselves First, That's Happiness

drive the car home and be quiet. *"Silence would be my best friend as I drove home,"* I thought to myself.

Well, that plan didn't work for very long because as soon as he got in the car, he tried to kiss me. I turned my face away from him, and of course, he asked me what was wrong. I started driving off and heading home. He kept asking me what was wrong and I just kept being quiet. He then told me to pull the car over. I kept driving and he kept on asking me what was wrong. Then I started crying. At this point, he grabbed the wheel of the car to try to pull it off to the shoulder of the road but I was pulling the wheel to stay on the road. Eventually, I gave in and pulled into a parking lot, which was about 10 minutes away from his job.

I screamed out at him " *I saw your ass kissing a woman outside your job!"*

Of course, he acted like an innocent little lamb and replied, *"Bae, what are you talking about?"*

I yelled, *"I got to your job early and I saw you!"*

He still denied it. Then I started back crying. He then walked around to the driver's side of the car and I moved to the passenger side and we rode in complete silence now; it's silent only because he's in shock that I saw him. Even though he's not telling me the truth, I could feel his energy of being caught in the act.

All I did was cry as he drove to our kids' daycare. Once we arrived at the daycare, I dried my eyes so my children wouldn't see me crying as he walked in to get them from the daycare. When we got home I just went into my usual mommy mode of cooking, getting clothes ready for the next day, giving our kids a bath. He helped as he usually did.

That night, we slept with our backs turned away from each other and in total silence. He didn't go to work for the next few days, but I still went to work. Even though I felt sad while at work, I could not financially afford to take off work. And I definitely could not afford to lose this job pending the outcome of my marital situation and the possibility of me being a single parent, which meant I needed to have some money coming in.

He tried to make small talk with me, but I only responded to him if the kids were listening to us. I didn't want our kids to be upset. After a few days of the silent treatment, he said that he would just quit the job. I agreed with him at the time. Keep in mind that he still had not admitted that it was him outside kissing that woman. He said that I probably thought it was him since I was looking from so far away. He swore up and down that it wasn't him. Now, any woman knows how her husband looks, even if it's from far away. *"I know your walk and your body shape,"* I reminded myself. He had to have thought I was a fool. But because of my naive mindset, I guess I was a fool at that time.

He was off work for about a week, using his vacation time. We then talked about him returning to work. We both agreed for him to go back to work, mostly because we needed the money. He promised me that he would stop wearing cologne to work and that he wouldn't iron anymore work clothes. Keep in mind that he still hadn't admitted to kissing that woman or to anything else, at all.

Fast forward 11 months later. We now have another baby, and she is six weeks old — which is old enough to start daycare. Our other two children were two and four years old. We have one son and two daughters, with our son being the oldest.

I had just finished maternity leave and would be back at work full-time. I have a new job with decent pay working at an insurance company which was approximately 45 minutes away from our house. He had been on his plant job for three years now, and had gotten a promotion and a raise in pay. We also just moved into a very nice three-bedroom rental home with a huge backyard for the kids to play in. And, oh, I forgot to tell you that we now have two fairly new cars. Life seemed great, and I was happy for the most part. Keep in mind that we were only 22 years old at the time so by most standards we were doing pretty good.

Ladies Love Yourselves First, That's Happiness

My new job was at the largest insurance company in the state of Alabama. It paid well enough money to allow me to only have to work that one job. No more part-time jobs for me, which meant less stress in my life and I liked the sound of that. I worked the day shift from 7:30 am to 3:30 pm. Meanwhile, he had to be at work by 2 p.m. and got off at 10:30 p.m. Most days, he would cook dinner for us before he went to work so all I would have to do when I got home was heat it up and give the kids a bath. No one was in school yet because we only had toddlers and a baby so there was no homework to deal with.

This next thing — the mail — had never even crossed my mind.

Normally our mail would be delivered around noon or 1 p.m. every day. That meant he would check the mail before he left for work and he would leave it on our kitchen counter. There was one day when he either forgot to check the mail or the mail carrier was running late that day. But something told me to go check the mail. I go outside and get the mail out of the mailbox. I immediately noticed that the home phone bill, which was a landline, was very thick. It looked like a small book. So of course, I opened it. There were several calls to a city which was nearly an hour from where we lived in Birmingham. The first thing I did was call the phone company. I told them that they have put a lot of calls on our phone bill that were not ours. The telephone representative told me that they were our calls. After going around and around with the representative for over 15 minutes I hung up and called my husband's job. I called the break room to have someone go get him to the phone. Because his job required him to walk around the plant all day, everyone knew he was flexible enough to be able to come to the phone.

So I get him on the phone and tell him about the large phone bill. Something in his voice sounded a little shaky to me. He said, *"Oh nah, they made a mistake. That's not our bill, they need to take that off our bill."*

I said, *"Yes, that's what I told them, but I'm about to call them back again."* Then I hung up with him.

But before I called the telephone company back, I dialed that number that I saw several times on my phone bill. A male voice answered the other end, *"Hello?"* He said.

I responded, *"Hello, I have some charges on my phone bill from this number, do you know anyone who lives in Birmingham?"*

The male voice responded, *"No, I don't know anyone who lives in Birmingham, they must have made a mistake at the phone company."*

I said *"Okay, thank you, that's what I figured too."* then I hung up.

I felt a tad bit better but I still had that uneasy feeling inside. So I started looking at the phone bill a little bit closer. I noticed that the phone calls were all made almost every day except for the weekends, and the times of the calls were all between 6:47 a.m. until around 1:15 p.m. Now, this was very important information because during those hours my husband was the only one at home. I would leave for work every morning at 6:45 a.m., so I could drop my children off at daycare on my way to work. He would leave home around 1:10 or 1:15 p.m. at the latest to get to work by 2 p.m. So I call the phone company back a second time. As I was talking to them, my husband kept trying to call me back, but I didn't answer him on the other end. This time I had a different telephone representative, and what they told me blew my mind!

The representative said, *"Ma'am, these are definitely your phone charges because this phone number has been on your bill for the past two months."*

My stomach started to feel very queasy. After I hung up with the telephone representative, I called the break room again and got my husband back on the phone. This time, before I could even say anything to him about what they had told me about that particular number being on our bill for the past two months, he started talking right away and in a hyper voice that I wasn't familiar with.

Ladies Love Yourselves First, That's Happiness

He said, *"Barry told me that he made those phone calls and he had them billed to our phone number as a third party."*

Barry is his brother and he also worked on the same job as my husband. Conveniently, he quickly puts Barry on the phone before I could even say anything.

Barry says, *"Hey Sis-in-law, yeah, I'm sorry 'bout that, I had those calls billed to y'all number and I meant to pay for them but didn't get a chance to."*

I finally got a chance to say something after all of their hyper over-talking lying asses were done.

I responded to Barry, *"Okay, so what's the phone number that you had billed to our number?"*

Barry answered, *"You know, Sis-in-law I don't even remember right now, but I can call you back with it."* I interrupted him then, *"Don't worry about it. Put your brother back on the phone."*

My husband gets back on the phone, and now his voice sounds even weirder. I tell him, *"The telephone operator said that this number has been on our bill for the past two months now. You didn't notice it before because you have been the one getting the phone bill out of the mailbox and paying it?"*

He responded, *"You know I didn't pay too much attention to it, and I just paid it."*

I said, *"Alright,"* and then I hung up as he was still trying to explain the lies.

I dialed that number on my phone bill a second time, and the same male voice answered again, *"Hello?"*

I responded, *"Hello, I'm sorry to bother you again, but are you sure that you don't know anyone in Birmingham because I called the phone company back and they said that this phone number has been on my bill for two months now."*

51

he replied, *"No, I don't know anyone in Birmingham, Ma'am."*

I continued, *"Does anyone else live there with you that could have made the calls?"*

He answered, *"The only people who live here with me are my fiancée and our son who is a small child."*

Then he asked me, *"Who lives with you, Ma'am?"* I said, *"It's me and my husband and three babies."*

He asked, *"Well what's your husband's name?"*

I said, *"Wayne Black."*

He then yelled through the phone, *"Wayne Black? That's the man who has been messing around with my fiancée! My mama works up there too and she told me about what everybody is talking about up at that chicken house, and how they are going out to the car having sex!"*

Nervously I asked, *"What is your fiance's name?"*

He said, *"Felicia."* I damn near fell off of my chair when I heard that name!

I will never forget that name, because almost a year ago when I saw my husband outside kissing the mysterious woman, I did a little investigation of my own. You see, that chicken house plant was the largest one in the state of Alabama at the time. There were hundreds or maybe even over a thousand people from Birmingham who worked there. It was a 24-hour operation, which meant that somebody knew somebody who worked there.

Since my husband's job requires him to always walk around the plant, most people who worked there knew him. I found a couple of people who knew him and both of those people gave me the same name as the woman that he was cheating on me with. The name they gave me was Felicia. They both gave the same description: a light-skinned woman. That's two separate people who gave

Ladies Love Yourselves First, That's Happiness

identical information on the mystery woman that I saw my husband hugging and kissing almost a year prior.

Here we are 11 months after the kissing scene that my husband had lied about and denied. Now it is apparent that he not only had an affair with Felicia but that the affair had never ended. I told Felicia's fiancé what I had seen the year before with them kissing outside the job and how my husband had lied and never admitted to anything at all. Felicia's fiancé said that she had been lying to him too, but that she did admit to having the affair. She only admitted it because his mother worked up there with her so she couldn't really get away with lying about it. She had also told him that they had broken it off a long time ago. But according to all these phone calls, it had not been broken off at all. I told Felicia's fiancé that I am now sure that their affair never stopped.

As I sat there and thought about it, I realized that my husband had started ironing those work clothes again and wearing cologne again. I could smell the cologne lingering in the air very faintly in our bathroom when I would get home from work in the evening with our kids. I didn't really notice what he was wearing since I was always at work when he left for work and I would usually be sleeping when he got home from work.

The previous year when he worked on the day shift and I had to take him and pick him up from work, I saw what he wore to work. A few times I did see his work clothes in our laundry hamper and I recalled that they had been ironed. He always did our laundry since I had to take our children to daycare and put them to bed at night. He did that to try to help even out the chores. I guess I was just too busy with our kids after work and just too tired to really pay close attention to these things. Plus, I had put it in the back of my mind and was trying to keep our family together and happy. I really wasn't looking for anything, or maybe I was denying what I might have seen in hopes that he was being faithful.

After talking to Felicia's fiancé on the phone for almost an hour, I hung up and I called my husband back in that break room once again. By now he had called me at least 20 times while I was on the other end with Felicia's fiancé, but I didn't click over to answer him. He came to the phone and I started screaming at him and cursing him out! *"You lying cheating ass motherfucking Bastard! you never admitted to anything last year and now I find out that it was your nasty ass out there kissing Felicia all along!" Her fiancé said that his mother works up there too and you've been sleeping with his fiancé all this damn time!!!!"* I kept yelling and cursing at his ass and didn't stop to listen to a word he had to say! Once I finished cursing and yelling at him, I just hung up on him!

Less than 30 minutes later, he was pulling up in the driveway at our house. He must have driven 80mph to get home that fast as his job was about 45 minutes to an hour away. The small town where the plant was located even had a 20 mph max speed limit! He had to have lied to his supervisor and told them that he needed to get home for some type of emergency for them to allow him to leave work so abruptly!

When he came through the door to our house I went up to him and slapped him as hard as I could and cursed him out! He grabbed my hands and started pleading with me and apologizing to me. The children were all crying, I was crying and cursing, just out of my mind with anger but mostly hurt, deep deep hurt like I had never felt before! To find out like this and to be betrayed like this and to be treated like nothing after giving so much! It was a feeling that I wish I never experienced! Here I am, always trying to overdo everything for the sake of this marriage and working all the time. I sometimes even worked two jobs to help this man and this is how I get repaid? Our infant child was barely four months old, and I'm already back at work! I had given up everything for this marriage and my little family because I felt like that was the right thing to do. I had absolutely no social life at all. I barely even went to the salon and would just do my hair and nails myself just to save money and help my family. To find out that this motherfucker had been cheating all along and spending money to impress a side chick and spending money on her just infuriated me! I knew that if my three babies had not been there at that very moment, I would probably still be in jail right now for what I would have done to him!

It took over an hour for me to actually sit down and calm down. Looking back now, I'm surprised I didn't have a stroke or a heart attack because my heart was beating so fast and I know my blood pressure was through the roof. God was with me that night because the outcome of that night could have been so different. The outcome could have left my children to be raised by family members and not their biological parents had I not calmed down.

He cried and begged me to please not give up on our family. For the next few months, he acted like a totally new person. Although I went and stayed with a family friend for the next few days, I eventually returned home.

Things were never the same after that night. I became an empty shell inside. I no longer had a real connection with my husband. I was just going through the motions, so to speak. I was lost and didn't want to put forth the effort to figure it out. I just couldn't understand how he could do this to me after I gave him a chance and allowed him to go back to that job where I know I saw him with my own two eyes kissing Felicia, and for him to hurt me even worse this time was just too much to deal with. Nothing he did nor said to me really mattered after that night. He eventually quit working at the chicken house, but the damage had already been done.

Six months later, I got another job at a different insurance company. This one paid even more than the last one and it was closer to my home. I was excited about this job because it was a fairly new company and there was the possibility of advancement very quickly. The only problem I had with this new job was that they lied to me when I was first hired. They told me that I needed to train on the evening shift, but that I would be working on the day shift. The evening shift ended up being my permanent shift which I did not like at all. I talked to my supervisor about it and he told me that I needed to stay on the evening shift for three to six months, then I could move to the day shift. I just gave in and said I would do the evening shift for the six months, but then I need the day shift because of childcare issues.

By now I had started shopping more and treating myself better than I ever had before. I was getting my hair and nails done on a regular basis. I started feeling much better about myself. My life was starting to feel happy again, aside from my marriage. Once I moved to the night shift, I started training with a nice-looking, well-groomed college-educated black man. We had a lot to talk about during our training. We talked about traveling, books, making more money, and many other things that we both had an interest in. Little did I know we were starting to get closer on a personal level. We started going out to eat at nearby restaurants on our lunch break and sometimes he would even bring me lunch to work, which was a pleasant surprise. Before I knew it, I was excited about going to work just to see him, and I think he felt the same way about seeing me at work too. Eventually, we started meeting up outside of work to eat and catch a movie or just sit at the park and talk.

One day he just kissed me out of nowhere. It made me feel wanted and special. That was the turning point in my life that gave me the thought that I could have something better than what I had at home. Deep down inside I felt like my marriage was already over and that the love that I once felt for my husband was long gone. We were only together because of our kids and a piece of paper that said we were married. Nothing else was there for real. A week after that first kiss with my trainer Shawn, we slept together. At first, I felt a little nervous because I knew I was still legally married, but overall I enjoyed everything about Shawn. I felt like he and I were way more compatible than my husband. We kept meeting up outside of work and eventually my husband did find out about the affair through some of my co-workers that were friends of his friend. We had several arguments about it and he asked me to quit my job and I said, *"No!"* Honestly, my husband couldn't really say shit to me because he knew he had fucked this marriage up when he decided to be a Whore and have an affair at work with that Felicia woman and continued on with it for over a year until I had to find out about it myself. He knew that he couldn't really push too hard because of that. Instead of quitting the job, I decided to separate from my husband. At first, I just moved out and stayed between family members and friends. I then rented an extended stay, and then I moved to Atlanta with Shawn. I started a new job at a large insurance company in Atlanta near the Buckhead area. Shawn was hired there as well.

New job, new city, new life. Although my husband had some problems with regard to the distance between Birmingham to Atlanta as far as visiting our children was concerned, nothing was going to stop me from my new life. My husband and I eventually worked out the visitation of our children over the course of six or seven months. He found somebody else after several months once he saw that I wasn't coming back to him. A year after I moved to Atlanta, I filed for divorce from my husband and had the papers sent to his new girlfriend's low income project apartment, which was where he was living. He signed the papers right away, because we had both moved on with our lives. I got married to Shawn shortly after my divorce was finalized. My ex-husband married his girlfriend shortly after I remarried.

Cadori

Wait for no one when it comes to fulfilling your dreams.
They either get on board or they get left behind.

Chapter 7

Me-Time & Self Reflection

Me time and self-reflection. I cannot stress to you how important this is to your self-care self-love journey. Your happiness requires that you spend quality time with yourself which means being alone. I know for me, I really wasn't raised to pour quality time into myself. I don't think a lot of people are raised to put in that alone time, especially women. We are natural nurturers. We're mothers, wives, sisters. Oftentimes, we carry the bulk of the emotional and even the financial responsibilities in our households. We tell ourselves that there is absolutely no time for ourselves.

It's all about what we tell ourselves - That we're too busy, that we have too much going on, that we just don't have the time, but in fact, we do have the time. If we don't think we have the time we need, then we have to make the time. We are the ones who are writing out the to-do list in most cases anyway, so why can't we put ourselves on that list?

If we continue to pour all of our energy and time into these jobs, our children, our husbands, our partners, our friends, our organizations, the different activities at our churches, and put ourselves on a back burner, we will pay the cost. We will come up short somewhere in our journey to happiness. Whether it is psychologically, physically, or spiritually, all of the pieces of the puzzles have to fit together for you to feel whole and happy. You put quality time and love into your relationship with your children. You put quality time and love into your relationship with your spouse or partner. The same goes for your friends, your church or organization, and your job. More importantly, you need to put quality time and love into yourself first! You are worthy and you deserve that quality time as well.

Up until about three or four years ago. I never really valued that *me-time* as much. There were a lot of things that happened in my life — from the loss of my oldest son to divorce after 24 years of marriage, two job losses, and other different life changes that were out of my control. Hence, I had to learn to treat myself well. I had to figure it out while I was getting mental health therapy. I really needed to start pouring into myself because my glass was completely empty. I should have been pouring into myself all along, but like I said, I just never stopped to think about myself because of how I was raised, then getting married and having a child right out of high school. All these years, I've been busy raising children and being a wife, and working on jobs, I just never thought about me. It's like I was on auto-pilot - self-care and self-love were not on board the flight.

When we make our to-do lists plans for the day or for the week, we have to put ourselves on that list as well. I've read many books on psychology over the years and I've watched a ton of self-care videos. I've gotten a lot of mental health therapy and I still currently get mental health therapy when I need it. All the different books and videos tell the same message — self-care and self-preservation are essential to our happiness and should be placed in the primary spot in our lives.

It's taken me most of my life to come to see that this is true. I had to learn this message the hard way when I was at one of the lowest points of my life. This was after I had been abandoned by my husband of 24 years who had suddenly walked out of our lives one day without saying a single word. I know now that he is a narcissist, but back then I didn't know what the hell was going on. After months of being deeply depressed and stressed, I finally decided to seek a mental health therapist to help me figure the shit out and start

Ladies Love Yourselves First, That's Happiness

rebuilding myself from the inside out. It was the battle for my sanity for real. If I didn't believe in God and my children at that time I would have given up on life. Thank God I had a flicker of hope in my body and the support of my children that helped to pull me through. I come to you from a place of compassion and truth to help you to realize that you cannot give everything you have to anyone. If you make sure that you are giving to yourself more than you are giving to others, you will not find yourself hanging on to life by a thread.

I'll tell you a great example of why we matter individually. For those of you who have flown on an airplane before, what are the instructions that the crew will tell you before taking off to fly? They say, *"In the event of an emergency, when these oxygen masks drop down from above your head, YOU NEED TO PUT YOUR OXYGEN MASK ON FIRST."* They didn't say to put on your child's, or your mother's or father's or spouse's oxygen mask first. Why is that important? Why should you put your oxygen mask on first, before you help assist someone else? It's because if the altitude drops, you would need oxygen. If you've put somebody else's oxygen mask on first, then you're going to pass out and be oxygen-deprived. When you're oxygen deprived, you will die! Hence, You won't be here to take care of your children or to help your spouse, parents, or anyone else for that matter. This oxygen mask instruction applies to everyday life as well. You should be taking care of yourself first in order to be able to take care of others.

During my 25 years in the healthcare field and being a registered nurse, I have personally taken care of far more women than men who have had heart attacks and strokes. Some of them died and some were left with lifelong disabilities. Most of their heart attacks and strokes were stress-related. Ladies, stress can Kill You! I repeat... Ladies, Stress can Kill You! It's better to be by yourself and happy than to have people in your life who are causing you stress, including family members. Who told you that you need someone in your life who is causing you stress? For what reason? It makes no sense at all to have people in your day to day life that are potentially harmful to your health and your very existence.

Cadori

News Flash: Stress is Controllable!

My hope is to inspire people, especially women, to pour into your cups until they are overflowing before you pour into anyone else. You need to hold people accountable in every relationship that you have so that you are not giving the most in the relationship all the time. Rather, they are equally pouring into your life as well and you are valuing yourself the most! You are just as important as anyone else on this planet! You have Value! You have Worth!

And it is time to put yourself FIRST!

*The more you focus on you the happier you will be.
Self care comes first.*

Chapter 8

Choose to be Happy & Protect Your Peace

One day, when my oldest son Dougie (rest in peace, son) was around 10 or 11 years old, he said out of nowhere, *"Mama, you should make yourself happy first."* I don't know where he got that phrase from, but he kept saying that to me from time to time throughout the rest of his life. I guess he would see me looking sad at different times in my life when I wasn't even aware that he was looking at me. Maybe he had noticed me stressing about something from always doing so much for them and not really doing anything for myself. His words never really hit me until after he passed away on October 12th, 2010. He was taken away from us in a motorcycle accident.

Shortly thereafter, I started remembering certain things that he had said to me because we were very close. We talked all the time and those words that he had said to me since he was a child stood out to me. It actually helped me find peace and move forward with life because they were his words from his mouth guiding me. After I had gotten grief counseling, I kept hearing him saying, *"Mama, you should make yourself happy first."* It was because he never really saw me do that. For the past 10 years, I've been working on myself and really trying to live my purpose and live my dreams that God gave me and be as happy as I can be. I've had to reinvent myself and I've had to let a lot of people go, including some family members, in order to live a peaceful and happy life.

The year 2017 was sad and depressing. It was when I can really pinpoint the most noticeable negative changes in my marriage, as far as being blatantly disrespected by my husband Shawn. He started the year off acting crazy around his birthday doing disappearing acts. He was a truck driver. His job would require him to leave town to take the deliveries to nearby cities. He would start conveniently staying an extra day or two, saying that his truck was broken down and that he had to wait there for the repair people to come and fix it or order a part that was required to get it back up and running. These breakdowns started becoming more frequent. This was not too out of the ordinary because I have family members who are over the road truck drivers so I know that there could be a lot of back-to-back mechanical problems. It wasn't something that I could really make a valid argument over. Plus, he was always sending me a picture showing something that was messed up on the truck to coincide with what he was saying at the time. My suspicion started to arise when he would purposefully make an argument over nothing right before he would leave for work. He would supposedly be upset at me. He would not answer his phone or text messages from me or from our children for as many as five days in a row. When he came back home, he would come into the house as if nothing had happened. He would always go into the kitchen and start cooking and talking to us as if he's been there every day. Neither I, nor our children wanted to argue with him and cause him to leave again so we just went with the flow to keep the peace in the household.

It was very stressful and very confusing because two years prior to that, his mother had passed away. He was fairly close to his mother, and he respected her. When she passed away, he didn't get any grief therapy or really even talked about her. I thought this was a warning sign and red flags because when my son passed away, I couldn't get in grief counseling fast enough. My son passed away in October 2010 and we were all in family grief counseling in January of 2011. The only reason we weren't in there before was because of the holidays and the counselors were all booked because of the holiday season. (I later found out that during the holidays people experience more grief and depression for the family members that they've lost). The holidays are just not a happy time for a lot of people. Well at least for me, I don't really even like celebrating Thanksgiving or Christmas after I lost my son. It's just very sad for me to think about all of those memories, childhood memories with him. I usually travel somewhere for the holidays to get my mind clear. I tried to sympathize with my husband after he lost his mom and I allowed his bad behavior towards me to continue just out of my trying to be understanding to him. Years later, I found out he was using my kindness for weakness because he was lying all of those times when he said that his truck had broken down. He made up those arguments to keep from answering his phone when he said that he had to work on certain days and travel out of town. Now I know that he was with other women all along since he lost his mom.

The biggest change that I noticed in 2017 was that he insisted that we renew our wedding vows on June 27th of 2017, which marked 24 years of marriage. We were married in Las Vegas Nevada. He wanted to go back to Vegas and renew the vows since that was where we originally got married. We had gotten into a couple of arguments leading up to the month before the renewal. At that point, I didn't want to go and renew the vows, but he begged and pressured me to go. I finally decided to do it. I found a nice gown before we left for Vegas, and he rented a nice tuxedo once we got there. We found a female minister to renew our vows. We chose to renew them standing underneath the famous Welcome to Las Vegas sign.

During the course of us renewing those vows, we were there looking at each other on this warm morning at 7:38am and I saw that he was crying a river of tears. I teared up a little bit too, but I remember looking into his eyes when we were renewing the vows, and I was thinking to myself, *"Why is he crying like this?"* He was more emotional than the first time when we got married. He shedded a few tears back then, but this time he seemed to be very overwhelmed with what seemed like grief. Something seemed a little off, but you just kind of brush it off, like a flash crosses your mind for two, three seconds. That's all it was, I thought, maybe he's crying because we'd been through a lot since the first time we got married. We had lost our son Dougie and now we've lost his mom. We had just gone through a lot emotionally and financially and had all types of changes over the years. Maybe he's thinking about some of those things I thought.

Approximately two weeks later, which was mid-July, I came home from work one day and I noticed that one of his cars which had been having some mechanical issues was no longer in the garage of our house. We had a two-car garage, and this particular car had been parked inside the garage for over a year. When I let the garage up, of course, I noticed that it wasn't there anymore. I remember going into the house and asking him, *"Where's the car?"*

He said, *"Oh, I found storage for it. Remember I've been telling you that I wanted to put it in a storage? Plus, we will probably move out of this house soon now that the kids are out of high school."*

I said, *"Yes, I remember you talked about getting a storage facility, but you never said you found one."*

It seemed a little strange, though he had mentioned getting storage before and he had also talked about downsizing to a smaller house or condo but nothing official. I just went along with it, but I did have an unsettling feeling in my stomach. I just couldn't figure out why he would have gotten a storage and not tell me about it.

About a month later, Hurricane Harvey hit Houston and surrounding areas with devastation. It was August, 25th, 2017. We had to evacuate from our neighborhood due to flooding and we ended up going to Dallas. A lot of people went to Dallas from the Houston area because of Hurricane Harvey. What was strange was that Shawn suggested we go there. We went there and checked into the hotel with our two youngest children, who had both graduated high school within the two years prior. After two or three days, he started an argument over something random and said he had to go

Ladies Love Yourselves First, That's Happiness

back to Houston and go to work. I thought they were off work like everybody else. He left us in Dallas because we couldn't get back to our neighborhood due to the flooding and because the power was still out there. We were in Dallas for about a week without him before he came back up. He went back to Houston and when he went back there, I noticed that a lot of times he would stop answering his phone. I didn't know what was going on and we got into several arguments on the phone because his lying ignorant ass was always doing manipulative things . He never gave any logical answers when I asked why he wasn't in Dallas with us and why his job was making him work when most things were still closed in the Houston area. He did, however, end up coming back to Dallas the last week that we were at the hotel.

The next few months he showed the same type of behavior that he had been doing on and off all year long. He even started bringing up old disagreements that we said were settled after we renewed our vows. I asked him why did we even renew our vows if he was going to continue starting arguments over nothing and bringing up old stuff? He said we shouldn't have renewed the vows. This was a shock and it was hurtful! He caused so much turmoil in our household for the next few months until it was beyond sanity. December came and as it was the last month of the year, I had no idea that it would be the last month of our marriage.

I came home from work on Thursday, December 22nd, 2017. We were supposed to go out to eat dinner — just the two of us. I got home and I noticed that his car was in the driveway but he wasn't in the house. The travel kit that he would take with him in his truck was on his side of the bathroom sink. I saw a package sticking out of it and I looked at it and it was a male enhancer sex capsule. He never had those before. About this time, My daughter yelled from the living room and asked me where her dad's motorcycle was. He usually kept it in the garage but it wasn't there. He walked through the front door about the same time I walked into the living room. He said, *"Come on, let's go eat."*

I asked, *"Where have you been and where is your motorcycle?"*

"Oh, I just took it up the street to get it fixed."

I asked, *"Where up the street? There's no mechanic in this area."*

He said *"Come on, let's go eat."*

I said, *"I'm not going to eat right now. How did you get back home? Your car is in the driveway and where did you go?"*

He sighed and said again, *"Let's go eat."*

I asked him why he had sex capsules in his kit. He lied and said that he uses them for us. I said, *"No, hell you don't! What the hell is going on with you?"* We argued for over an hour and I finally went to bed. I just remember crying myself to sleep.

The next morning he apologized for yelling at me the night before, but said nothing about the sex capsules nor the motorcycle. I was about to leave for work, so he hugged me and we kissed goodbye. Little did I know that it would be the last kiss before he moved out. I went to work and I called him on my break, and he didn't answer, I texted him, he didn't respond, I called several times throughout the day, same thing, no answer. Our children called and texted him throughout the day as well, yet he still didn't respond. I got home from work and he's not there and he still hasn't called.

The next morning I wake up after another sleepless night and a voice whispers in my ear, *"Go look in the closet."* I walked into the closet and saw that all his clothing but three shirts and one pair of shoes were gone. I looked under his side of the bed where he kept some of his shoes, and they were all gone too. I walked into the kitchen and looked under the counter where we kept the pots and pans that I mostly bought for him because he loved to cook, and they were all gone too. I walked to the garage where we had storage boxes full of things that we couldn't put in the house, and all of his boxes and things in the garage were gone too. I went and sat down on the sofa and I called our two youngest children who still lived with us into the living room. They sat down and I told them, *"Your dad has moved out."* They couldn't believe it. I told them to go look in our closet and look under the kitchen sink and look in the garage, and see that all of his things are gone. They went and looked and saw that he had indeed moved out. We all just sat there in a state of shock. Later, I cried and I think my daughter cried too. I just couldn't believe that the person that I thought I knew would leave without saying a word to any of us.

Over the next couple of weeks, I went searching for some answers because he wasn't answering any of our calls or text messages. I figured out his passwords and got into his Facebook account and found multiple women in his inbox that he had been sleeping with over a period of years. I got into his phone records and discovered even more women.

Come the second week of January, he started answering my text messages with many hateful responses. He still wouldn't talk on the phone. On February 25th, he sent a happy birthday text message to me. I responded and said thanks, but he still wouldn't talk on the phone nor answer any questions in the text messages. In the first week of March, my kids and I moved out of the house. It was a very painful move because this wasn't how it was supposed to be. I took a travel nursing assignment in another state for a few months. The change was good for all of us.

In August 2018, I was able to hire a private detective to put the pieces of this puzzle with my husband together. By now, he had tried to reconcile with me twice. Both times lasted about two weeks each because he did not want to talk about why he moved out of the house nor where he had been all of those months. His response was always, *"That's in the past. If we love each other then we should just move forward because we can't change the past anyway."* That answer didn't work for me nor did the fact that he didn't want to talk about any of it. I hired a private investigator and I got all of the answers that I needed to file for a divorce. But first I had to go get checked for every STD known to man because what the investigator found out was that this man had been having unprotected sex with God only knows how many women. I had to wait several days to get my results back. I was praying and crying every day that I didn't have any diseases. When I got back to the Doctors office to get my results, they told me to have a seat. It was as if I was moving in slow motion as they read the results out loud.

"Everything is negative." All I could do was say, *"Thank you God!"*

I just sat there for 20 minutes just crying. I got up and left the Doctors office and I made a left turn straight to the lawyer's office and filed for a divorce from that manipulative lying ass, cheating ass, coward ass, fucking Narcissist! I have not spoken to my ex since I hired the private investigator. That's been over two years now. My divorce was finalized on August 19th, 2019.

Since I decided to file for the divorce, I've been happier and more at peace than I've ever been!

YOU are enough all by yourself!
God created you individually with everything that you need to be happy.
*YOU are One of a Kind, a **MASTERPIECE**!*

Chapter 9

Distance Yourself From Negative People, Including Some Family Members

Distancing yourself from negative people, including some family members. This is a taboo topic but it's a much-needed one because negative people can cause unnecessary stress and pain in our lives. We have the power to step away from people and situations if we choose to. Continuing to be around these types of people will only cause us more pain. We feel pain when people do hurtful things to us, especially if we did not do anything hurtful to them to cause that pain.

I dedicate this chapter to the people who have lost their lives while staying in a toxic relationship because they didn't know how to break free. I'm sure there are tons of people out there who can relate to this topic.

I believe that when you're on a journey to living your purpose and ultimately becoming happy, you're going to notice people from every direction who are just negative and who will not support you. You have to accept the fact that it's okay to love people from a distance. I personally have people that have been close friends to me, as well as some family members who have been non-supportive and mean-spirited as well. That non-support alone is a red flag that they are not only jealous of you but they are envious as well!

It's very dangerous for us to be around envious people. To me envy means that not only are they jealous of you, but they believe in their heart and soul that you have something that they could NEVER have! And it doesn't matter if what they believe is even true or not, the fact is that they believe it, so it's very real to them! That's why it's very dangerous to be around envious people! There are times when you have people who are close to you or related to you and they say that they love you, but you have products, or projects, or a business and they have never supported you. Even when you had something for sale for $1, they still never supported you! Get as far away from those people as you can, and do it as quickly as you can! On top of that, those same people are constantly saying negative things about what you're doing and spreading lies about you day and night. You would never be happy when you're around those people because they will not allow it. And they will do everything in their power to keep other people from supporting you as well.

I started on my self-healing journey about seven or eight years ago. Which was a couple of years after I lost my oldest son, Dougie, to a motorcycle accident on October 12th, 2010. The loss of my son was very devastating and it changed my life forever. I never go a day without thinking about him. I've learned after losing my son that it is the greatest loss when you lose your child! Parent and child relationships are the closest on earth. No one expects to outlive their child, and you don't expect to lose a child either! It's the hardest pain ever, I believe. After losing my oldest son— someone whom I loved and I gave birth to — really made me put things into perspective with life in general. One of those things that I put into perspective was the intolerance of people who don't support you and who are negative. Sometimes — in fact, oftentimes, they go hand in hand.

I started calling people out. First were family members that didn't support me — didn't really call me to check on me or anything. Most people in my life and my family, or whom I have been acquaintances with, are actually the same people who I've helped more than once. I've given them my advice, money, support, and

Ladies Love Yourselves First, That's Happiness

time. I've learned that no matter what you do for other people it doesn't mean that they will do the same thing for you.

The more I recognize the people who are negative and non-supportive, and the more that I distance myself from them, then the happier I've become. That's simply because you don't have to listen to all that crap and lies that they tell you anymore. You also no longer have their negative energy around you anymore. These are just a few things that some of those negative ass non-supportive people used to say to me when I allowed them to be near me:

"Anyway, why are you doing this?"

" That won't work because it's already been done before."

"Somebody else already tried that and it didn't work."

"Oh! you're trying something else again."

"You're doing too much."

"Why are you trying to do all of this?"

" How are you going to support this?"

"I think you just need to focus on one thing."

It was always the same type of negative conversations over and over again. When you talk to them, you can't even share your good news nor your plans with them because they're going to talk negatively to you and end up making you feel bad. Ultimately, you have to get to a point where you are courageous enough and fearless enough to actually distance yourself from these types of people. It does not matter if they are blood-related to you at all. Sometimes the people who are closest to you will hurt you the most!

Just ask yourself, why do I need to hear negative things from them and not have their genuine, heartfelt support, especially if you've given that support to them? When you distance yourself from them, don't be afraid to block their numbers, or don't give them your new number when you change your number. Distance yourself. Hide their pages on your social media so you're not consumed with their negative energy. You're not going to be able to survive and be as strong as you need to be mentally if you keep dealing with them. They're not bringing anything positive or supportive to the table in your life.

I just think that once you start becoming more self-aware and you start valuing yourself more, you will be able to identify the people who are not supportive of you and who are very negative in your life. It doesn't mean you don't have a love for that person if they are your family member or close friend, rather, you have to learn to love them from a distance. You have to learn to be okay with that because you can't change anyone but yourself, **and Do Not allow other people from the outside looking in to say things like:**

"Well, that's your family."

"You shouldn't treat them that way."

"You should go around your family."

People aren't in your shoes. They're not in your headspace. They're not in your body. They don't feel your emotions. You have to stand up for yourself. You don't have to explain anything to anybody or prove anything to anybody. **But you do need to stand up for yourself and say, "NO!"**

"No", I will no longer be treated with disrespect.

"No", I will no longer be taken advantage of.

"No", I will no longer be mentally abused.

"No", I will no longer accept non-support and negativity in my life."

The word *"NO"* can be your best friend when it comes to fully appreciating yourself and your time and your energy.

Ladies Love Yourselves First, That's Happiness

•Choose to handpick the people that you want to be close to you so you can be happier.

•Choose to be around people who want to be around you.

•Go where you are celebrated and not just tolerated.

•Don't argue with anyone - just let your actions speak louder than your words.

•You are powerful beyond your imagination. Combine that with self-love and knowing that your worth is golden!

Trust me, when you learn to love yourself first you will truly experience the peace and happiness that you deserve.

I know I have!

***Learn to say "NO"**
**People will continue disrespecting you
if you allow it. Stop allowing it!
Stop letting people use you for convenience.***

Chapter 10

Manifest What You Want

Manifest what you want. It has to be intentional. You have to have a few things in place to properly manifest. First of all, you need to believe whatever it is that you would like to manifest. You need to believe it as if it has already happened so that you can walk in it. Then you need to have faith. Faith is the idea and the belief that it has already happened. They're not thoughts of anything other than positivity, and the things that will help to bring what you want into fruition which makes it a reality. Next, you need to do the work, because faith without work is dead. You need to be walking in what you want to manifest — actively doing things so that it can become a reality. You need to act as if you already have received it! That means you're happy about it! You feel it, and it will happen! It has *already* happened!

I'll tell you a story about manifestation this year during the pandemic. Even with all of the changes that are going on almost daily and the fear of the unknown or what is to come, I have remained so positive that everything that I wanted and had spoken of going into the year 2020 has become a reality!

And the things that I've manifested are still happening to this very date!

I started out the year and I made a post that I'm going to manifest what I want, and that's what happened. When the pandemic happened, it didn't matter to me. I was still thinking positively. While I've had to make a few adjustments and changes to some things because of the quarantine requirements, I've still been able to bring those ideas and things that I wanted to fruition. It's because I speak positivity about things, and I speak life into things and situations in order to bring things into reality. I sat down and wrote down the steps that were different from the initial steps that I had planned to bring the things that I want into reality.

One of the things that I had on the to-do list at the beginning of the year was to complete my book that you're reading right now and to have a huge book event initially planned for April 2020. When the pandemic hit, I had recently made the deposit on an event center that I was going to host the book event. I had also made deposits for the people who were coming to speak at the event, as well as a DJ and entertainers to perform and sing.

Here comes the pandemic and everyone has to quarantine, self-isolate, stay at home, and not go to work. We initially put the event on hold like everyone else had to do. But after the dates for when things might open back up kept changing, we had to keep putting it on hold until I decided to go a different route. All of the places that we normally would visit and things that we normally do didn't fully open. I decided to release the book and do a virtual book event. I never got upset about it. I never worried about it one bit, because worrying is negativity. I did not want to bring any negativity to something that is positive and something that is meant to help other people and change their lives for the better. I did not want to bring that negativity into this realm. I transferred it to a virtual book event, which is now happening and before us. I know that it will be very successful and it will do exceedingly above and beyond what I prayed for because God is in the driver seat! Everyone has a tablet or a computer or a smartphone so I can still reach people and get this message to them. Look, you're reading this right now! You see that you can still have a positive impact on the people that you want to impact.

Ladies Love Yourselves First, That's Happiness

I put all of my energy and positivity into the virtual book event and it has been wonderful! The response has been amazing, even from just telling people about the book that's coming out — they have been so excited!

The second thing that I spoke and I wanted to manifest at the beginning of this year 2020, was a certain income level and it had nothing to do with the pandemic. I spoke of it at the beginning of February 2020. Before the pandemic started, I told God, I would like to make X amount every week. What God did was he put forth things in front of me that I could choose from to make that happen. I made the choices that would make it happen. When the choices came to me, I chose what I had already wanted to happen - what I had already spoken into fruition. Guess what God did instead of giving me what I asked for as weekly pay? He tripled that amount because I believed it! I felt it!

I could feel it all over me when I was thinking about it at the very beginning. I could see it too! Then I spoke it. I wrote it down on paper and I read it out loud, and I read it often. That's another thing that you should do — write it down! If you want to manifest your thoughts and you have faith, then write it down. What you believe to be true, write it down! Then you can look at it and you can constantly read it. You can feel it. You can speak it. When you're manifesting you don't need to discuss it with anyone else. Honestly, what you want for yourself, and what you are manifesting is between you and your energy, and God. You don't need anyone else's energy or thoughts or comments about *your* manifesting! It's all within *you*! You only need your ideas, thoughts, and beliefs. Your positivity, joy about it, work, faith, and everything else is within you!

Manifestation and the power of the tongue are real. What you speak is real. What you believe, have faith in, work toward, visualize, speak, walk-in, and write down is real. You should start doing it right here right now. You can manifest anything that you want! In fact, it's already happened. You just haven't seen it yet before your eyes, but it's already done.

Cadori

You absolutely have the power to manifest what you want!

Ladies Love Yourselves First, That's Happiness

YOU have the POWER to speak it into existence!

Chapter 11

Woman Warrior

I believe that within each of us is a Warrior that's waiting for us to wake her up! She's right there all along with all of her super natural greatness to be used when we choose to walk into the purpose that God has created us for. If we would dare to be by ourselves for a little while, and be silent enough to hear the calling on our life, she begins to awaken.

Once we know our purpose then the path that is set before us is the journey to our true Greatness. We will be able to fulfill our purpose because the Woman Warrior that is within us has now been awakened to help us to get there. *She is Fearless, She is Courageous, She is Unstoppable, She is a Fighter, She is a Goddess, She is Powerful, She is Confident, She is Compassionate, She is Brave, She is Strong, She is Heroic and She is Love!* And she is within each one of us! Believe it and Live it!

Repeat after me,

I AM A WOMAN WARRIOR!

Cadori

Listen to your inner voice.
It's your soul speaking to You

Chapter 12

Stand in Your Power & Never Give Up

You have power. You have worth. You should learn to love yourself first. It cannot be said enough times for you to hear that the power that you have within yourself is all you need to be great! Once you realize that you truly have power, then you start treating yourself better and you stop letting other people control and manipulate you and treat you less than you deserve. I've had my fair share of challenges in my life to work through, and I'm sure that there have been many challenges that have probably happened in your life as well.

I learned a lot after getting some mental health counseling, combined with spending time alone and learning to fully love myself and being truthful with myself about different issues in my life. I had to take accountability and own up to the fact that I stood by and kept quiet about some important decisions in my life that were being made by other people. I learned to be truthful with myself and accept that, in the past, I was simply not confident enough at those times in my life. Maybe I just did not want to go through the pain that would have come with making a different decision about something I was kind of sure about at the time. Guess what happened when I let other people make important decisions for me? I ended up having to go through even worse pain than if I had followed my internal voice about the issue in the first place.

Let me give you an example of a painful decision that I endured years earlier and saved time and got to a better place in my life a lot sooner. I've always been a people pleaser my entire life. I have a kind loving heart, to the point where I tolerated people walking all over me and being very disrespectful to me. I'm talking about people who were very close to me as some of my family members and some close acquaintances or co-workers. I would allow people to put all of the pressure on me to travel out of town to visit them for years and years, even from way back when my children were small, those same family members or acquaintances never visited me at all! I guess my mind was mostly on my children just not being able to know who their family members were or be as close to them as I thought they should be. I would always think about how when I was growing up, and I never really got to visit my cousins and aunts and uncles, and was never really close to them, and I didn't want my children to experience the same pain that I felt from that. As a result, I took on that heavy burden of being the sacrificial lamb for the sake of being close to family members, in-laws, exes. My children got to visit family, but guess who was the one making those visits happen? Me, and me alone! It never ever dawned to me that for over 15 years, that I was the only one who was putting in the time and effort to travel over eight hundred miles each way, whether by car or bus or plane to visit these selfish ass people! Only a handful of them visited us maybe five or six times over a span of 15 years or so! They visited and traveled to other places, but not to my house. I just never stopped to think about that shit until the past 10 years of my life which was after my son passed away. I'll tell you this, once a person who is very close to you dies, you start to really look at the people around you and their true character. Once you start mentally and spiritually growing in your life, you look at people for who they truly are from the inside out. You start looking at the intentions of people, which is in essence the real reason that people act the way they act. They can no longer hide behind words because you will forevermore make them do their part in the relationship too. You learn that you no longer have to listen to them try to make you feel like you are the only one who can get in a car and drive to see them, but that they can get in a car

Ladies Love Yourselves First, That's Happiness

and drive to see you just as easily. You no longer allow them to make you feel bad about not coming around for holidays because they can come and spend some holidays with you just as well. You no longer feel like you have to call them on their birthdays or other special occasions and buy them gifts just to make them feel special but that they too can call you and buy you gifts to make you feel special too. You no longer feel that if you don't come around that they will talk bad about you because guess what? Even when you have come around them all those years before, they still found something bad to say about you anyway. You no longer let them tell you that someone is going through a hard time and you should call them and offer them support and words of encouragement because you now know that they have never called you to even check up on you and see how you were doing. **You no longer feel bad about treating people exactly the same way that they treat you!** You no longer feel like you are the one that has to hold all of these relationships together just because you are a kind and giving person. You no longer even care what anybody feels about anything because you know that your feelings are just as important about things as anyone else feeling on the planet! You start to feel your power and use your power to make yourself feel that happiness that you have longed for your whole life and that you looked for someone else to give to you. You now know that no one can give you the kind of real happiness that you can give to yourself. You know that the important thing is that you are happy with yourself and that's all you need along with God by your side.

You now know that people are just people and that they can have good intentions or bad intentions, whether they are related to you or not. I always look at the Bible verse that relates to Cain killing Abel. They were family — they were brothers! Sometimes, your own family can be your worst enemy and they get to hide behind a word called family. They can hurt you deeply just by saying certain words. Don't be fooled by the word called *family,* just look at how the people are treating each other. Is there genuine care and love? Do they equally give to each other and pour into each other's lives or do you have one-sided relationships where one person is doing all the giving, calling, and traveling to see each other? Look closer and deeper into those relationships called family. I've had some people who have come into my life and have treated me with nothing but pure love and genuine care and concern and a mutually giving relationship for years. They are not related to me by blood, but they are indeed my family. I can call on them with confidence faster than I can call some of my family members. It was a very hard pill to swallow when my oldest son passed away, and only a few family members called or visited me because I live in a different state than most of them do. It was very painful, and it's still painful to this very day. Every year my son still has his birthday, he still has his *angel-versary*, we still have to make it through the holidays without him being here. On those special days, I didn't even get a call or a text message from the family. And it's still the same way to this very day. It does not matter about the word family - what matters is how people treat you in the end. On those special days, I do get calls and text messages from my Angel Mom Group members, and I do get calls and text messages from those dear friends. I am so thankful to God for them! I still have a love for all of my family because I'm not a hateful person. I wish them all well, but I just don't really deal with a lot of them because they have caused me so much pain in my life. If there is to ever be any type of close relationship with them then they will have to do most of the traveling and giving at this point because I am done with it. That door is locked. I won't put myself in a position for anybody to hurt me again. The blindfolds are off. I'm still the same loving caring and giving person that God created me to be, but now I use wisdom and discernment when dealing with people. I have my eyes wide open now.

I want to close this chapter by giving you some inspiration and motivation with some examples of how no matter how hard life has been for you that you can take control of your life by the decisions that you make and how you choose to deal with adversity. I've had to make some tough decisions about family and jobs and even recently about getting out of a marriage that was slowly destroying my very being because of the stress and constant lies, and

Ladies Love Yourselves First, That's Happiness

manipulative behavior that my then husband was doing. I had to make the decision that was best for me because I realized that my life is worth more than what I was going through with him. I had to make the choice to file for the divorce and live the rest of my life more peacefully and with true happiness. Otherwise, I would still be married to him right now because he wasn't going to file for the divorce. I didn't need anybody on the planet to tell me anything about how I know he made me feel inside. It's about being true to yourself at the end of the day! Every relationship that you have in your life is going to be with people (well mostly, because I know that our pets have their way of communicating with us too, and they are loyal.) You have to be honest with yourself and decide if these people mean you well —if they are bringing positivity to your life or negativity. What is your inside voice, which is your soul talking to you, what is it telling you? The more you spend time with yourself the more you hear your inner voice speaking to you. You will begin to listen to it and know that it will guide you to the best decision for you.

The Power that is inside of you can propel you through some of the most difficult times in your life. You just have to be willing to use your power. It's called Your Will, and your Desire. No one can give that to you because you already have it inside of you. You were born with it. Now, you will find in life that people will try to take your power away from you. One way that they can take your power away is by speaking for you when you can speak for yourself. Another way that people try to take your power away from you is by making decisions for you. In each of those examples of how people will try to take your power away from you just take a few moments and think about it. When people speak for you and you actually have something to say about whatever it is that they are speaking for you on, how does that make you feel? Think about people who make a decision for you about something that you actually know what you want to do. How does that make you feel when that made their decision for you? You will probably feel powerless. See how that works? You do have power whether you believe it or not, but you have to be confident enough to use it. You'll get there. It just

Cadori

takes time to get used to it because you have never really used it before. Trust me, I know because I was once right where you are. Remember one of your first steps in using your power is getting comfortable telling people, "*No!*"

The power that we have, when we decide to use it, will help us to get through some of the worst times of our lives. I'm only telling you this because life is uncertain. When you go through something challenging, you will need to remember that you still have power. In every situation in life, someone has to make a decision about something. Try your best to remember that you still have power. I've taken care of so many patients over the years that it would take months to tell you all of the impactful stories of some of the bravest people that I've ever met in my life. But I'll just sum up a few messages that I learned throughout my personal life and the lives of the patients that I've taken care of:

-You still have choices. Even if it's a terminal illness, you can decide however many more days you have to live.

- I'm going to be as happy as I can be for the rest of my days.

-I'm going to do something I didn't get to do before, like read that book that I always wanted to read or listen to it in an audiobook.

- I want to eat something I never got to eat or my favorite foods every day or my favorite drink or milkshake or candy or whatever you choose to eat.

-I'm going to watch my favorite movies or a movie that I always wanted to see.

-I'm going to wear something that I love or something new that I want.

-Anything that you can think of, but make it about you and what you choose. Because even in the face of death you can still have the power over some things no matter how small, it's still your choice to make.

I recognized my power at the most tragic time in my life when my oldest son Dougie passed away. I had to immediately make

Ladies Love Yourselves First, That's Happiness

decisions about his funeral because I was his mother and he was not married. I was devastated, but I knew that no one else could do what I had to do. No one else had my voice. I had to stand in it and speak up for what I knew my son would be proud of me doing. I actually had to argue with the funeral home director because he tried to make a decision about my son's funeral that was not his to make. I wanted my son to have an open-casket funeral but the director said it had to be a closed casket. On top of that, he said that I couldn't even see my son's body because it was not good for me to look at him that way. After my mother-in-law told me how they still got to view her aunt and uncle despite how badly their bodies were, I gained the courage to stand up and speak up. She also reminded me, *"Now Cathy, this is not something that you can do over, once the casket is in the ground there is no turning back, so think about that."* That was all I needed to hear to stand up at that moment and speak out. It's true that God will place people around you at the right time when things are happening in your life, but you have to be able to recognize it at that specific time. And at that specific time, it was my mother-in-law. I called the funeral home back and I said, *"Hello this is Bobby Brown's (that's my son's birth name but we called him Dougie) mom and I want to see my son's body and I want to have an open-casket funeral, too."*

The Funeral home guy says *"Ma'am we already told you that your son's body can't be viewed."*

I said, *"Is it because it can't be viewed, or because y'all don't want to get it ready to be viewed."*

The Funeral home guy replies, *"Now, Ma'am I don't want to argue with you but we have to follow rules here."*

I cut him off as he tried to continue, *"Rules? what rules? My son is dead and you have his body and I haven't even seen it! How the hell do I know if that's even my son! You all are very insensitive and you think I'm a fool but if you don't get my son's body ready for me to see right away then I'll be headed there with the police and have my son's body*

Cadori

taken to another funeral home across town who I've already spoken to who will get my son ready and let me view his body!"

Less than 3 minutes later the funeral home director calls me, *"Mrs. Cathy, we will have your son's body ready for you to view, but give us a few hours please."*

I said, *"Thank you, we will be there at 3:30 then."*

Had I not used my power and spoke up and fought for what was right for my son and for us, even in the face of that tragedy, none of us would have gotten to see my son and have the kind of closure that we needed or deserved. Had I not gotten out of my raw, sad emotions and rose to the occasion, I would have regretted it for the rest of my life! It was something that only I could have done and would have done. My son's father was fine with a closed casket funeral, but that was his choice. I'm the mother and I carried him and gave birth to him. It was my choice to see my son, and know that it was him in that casket, and it was my choice to have an open-casket funeral. After they went and actually did the work that they were already being paid to do on my son's body, he looked just fine. You couldn't really tell that anything had happened to his face at all.

I'll leave you with this inspiration about your choices and your power.

Thank you all so much for buying my book and for investing in your own happiness. Keep going, and you will get to where you want to be. You are special and you are one of a kind so never forget that! My hugs and love to each of you!

I was reading something the other day on Instagram and it stuck with me because of the way that it was worded. It was very powerful. It talked about two sons who were raised by an alcoholic father. One of the sons ended up being an alcoholic as well. Someone asked him what happened to you to make you become an alcoholic?

He said, *"I watched my father."*

The other son who was raised in the same house by the same alcoholic father never drank any alcohol at all. He didn't even drink at social events.

They asked that son the question, *"What happened to you that made you not drink any alcohol ever?"*

He said, *"I watched my father."*

What does that tell you? Depending on how you look at things will determine the outcome in your life, you have two sons raised by the same father in the same house and their lives turned out completely different. The one who is an alcoholic doesn't keep a job. He doesn't have the income to support himself most of the time, because everything goes to alcohol. He has to live with people, and sometimes he even sleeps on the street. He doesn't have a car or even a bicycle for transportation. Meanwhile, the other son, who was so affected just as deeply by his father's alcoholism is doing quite well. He has a very nice income, a career job, owns his home, has two cars that are paid for, and he travels often. In this example, each son got to choose how they would allow their upbringing to affect the rest of their lives. We all get to choose the life that we desire to have. You have the power and you can use that power if, and when, you want to use it.

You can live the life that you want to live. You can truly be happy if you want to be happy, because that's a choice, just like everything else that we're doing. When things are out of your control, you pray about it. You give it to God and you make the best of that situation, but that should not stop you from anything, nor make you give up on yourself. Surround yourself with positive people, and read those positive affirmations and quotes. Do you have a mental health therapist? You can even do mental health therapy over the phone, or on the internet now, because there is FaceTime and Zoom and many other sites to choose from. It doesn't have to be in-person anymore. So there is no excuse at all. Make sure you FILL your cup up until it's overflowing, before you start pouring into

Cadori

anybody else and never, ever, ever give anyone your power and never ever, ever give up on yourself!

Believe in Yourself
Even if no one else on the planet believes in you!

Bonus Chapter #1

Choose To Be Respected Rather Than Liked

One of the most demeaning things we can do as women is seek someone else's approval of us by any means necessary. Oftentimes, just to feel accepted or to fit in with other people, we compromise our integrity. Our integrity can even be compromised by family members, friends or even our significant others or our husbands, by allowing people to repeatedly disrespect us. I chose to write on this topic because for years I allowed people to walk all over me. I am naturally a kind and giving person, but have learned that the saying is true that a lot of people take kindness for weakness. It really is such a shame, but through all of my heartache from being run over and backed over by people being mean spirited and disrespectful to me, I have managed to become much stronger mentally than I ever thought I could be. It took longer than it should have for me to reach this fearless point in my life, but never- theless I have arrived and I will never let anyone else disrespect me.

I was a Charge Nurse several years ago in a large healthcare facility in Houston, Texas. As I said before, I am naturally kind and giving to others. Well, being in a leadership role on any job means a bunch of people will be coming to you with a multitude of problems and issues on any given day while working. I remember one day in particular (this is the day that I decided that I would rather be respected than liked) a co-worker came to me complaining about a patient care assignment. This particular person had known me for two or three years, and knew that I was always fair when I made patient care assignments, and that I was willing to help anyone with their work if I was not busy myself. This person was also someone that I would call my friend and we sometimes ate lunch or dinner together at work and shared stories about our lives with each other. Well, on this particular day, this co-worker/friend of mine did not like her assignment and wanted me to change one of her patients for a much easier patient, medically speaking. If I would have changed the assignment, it would mean that another co-worker would have three medically challenged patients instead of two, which was what each coworker had that night. So I told my co-worker that the assignment would not be fair to our other co-worker, at all, and that I could not and would not do that to our other co-worker. That did not make this co-worker happy. In fact, I even contemplated taking this co-worker's patient and giving her one of my easier patients to ease the palpable tension, but this would have put me in a bind since I was in the leadership role that night. Furthermore, if any other co-worker would have needed my help I would not have been able to come to their aid due to the attention the heavy assignment would have required. And per our unit rules, I was not supposed to take on a heavy assignment as a Leader on the unit in the first place.

I fought with myself a few hours into the shift about this dilemma. Finally, I decided that night that I would rather be respected by my peers and co-workers than liked. Although that particular co-worker/friend of mine was livid at me the entire shift for not swapping her patient care assignment, I felt a sense of peace internally, because I was doing what was right, not only by the other co-worker, but also by the patient. If I had changed that assignment and either took the patient myself or given the assignment to the other co-worker, I would have felt horrible inside as the only reason would have been because, "I didn't want my co-worker/friend to be mad at me."

After that night, I made my mind up completely to choose to be respected over being liked in every aspect of my life. As a result, I

Ladies Love Yourselves First, That's Happiness

have not allowed anyone else to run over me and treat me any way that they feel. Whenever we let people talk to us and treat us with disrespect and we accept that, it teaches them to continue disrespecting us in the same way. We cannot let anyone make us feel like we are not worth respect. We have to first treat ourselves with respect, then we have to show others respect, then we can demand it from others. I have also learned that if your friends, co-workers, or family members do not respect you, then they probably really don't like you either. Like and Love are two different things. You can love someone and not like them. It's not about people liking you anyway. If you can't be your true self around people because you don't feel they will accept you, then what kind of relationship is that anyway. If people like you just the way you are and they show you respect, that's the truest relationship. If people don't like you, want you to change, or be what they want you to be then that's a fake relationship. You will always feel uncomfortable not being yourself when you are around those types of people.

Choose today, that you would rather be respected than liked if it comes down to it.

As I look back over the years and evaluate relationships and things that happened, when I think about disrespect a multitude of relationships immediately come to mind. Unknowingly, all those times I was being overly-nice, gracious and kind in these relationships to these people, I was actually teaching them that I accepted their disrespect and I welcomed their treatment towards me, because I did not stand up for myself or ever even say anything to any of them about how I felt when they did or said things to me that I didn't like or deserve. I was teaching them to treat me the exact way they were already practicing. It's a sad situation when I look back and see that my self esteem was so low that I accepted bad behavior with a smile, but not anymore my friends. I have learned that painful lesson and now I am encouraging others to never sit back and accept any type of negativity. Directly address the person who is mistreating you, because they would not want or accept that type of bad behavior if the shoe was on their foot.

Bonus Chapter #2

Spending Time With Yourself

I can't tell you how critically important this is to your self esteem! Because most of us were not taught the value of getting to know and love ourselves enough to spend time alone, we started out as pre-teens and teenagers always having someone with us and in our face every hour of the day! We have become dependent on other people to make us feel fulfilled and ultimately we believe that everyone else is responsible for our happiness when that is not true at all. Each one of us is the Most Responsible for Our Own Happiness! Not our friends, not our children, not our family mem- bers, not our boyfriends, wives, significant others or husbands. They are the Most Responsible for their Own Happiness but We are the Most Responsible for Our Own Happiness.

Now, our friends, children, family members, wives, significant others, boyfriends or husbands can certainly add to our happiness, but they are not more responsible for our happiness than we are and we are not more responsible for their happiness than they are. You may ask "Why?" Well, it's very simple. No two people have the same brain. Why should I feel like I can make someone feel good about themselves more than they can, if my brain doesn't work in the exact same way as theirs? I would not even be able to assimilate information exactly like they do to figure out how they achieve happiness, what makes them feel happy, and what makes them feel good about themselves. It's impossible. I can certainly motivate and inspire other people, but I cannot make them change the way they feel internally. People have to do that for themselves.

This is why it is urgently important, imperative, and essential to learn to spend time alone and fall in love with yourself first, early in life!

If you never did that, then now is the time to start planning out your day, putting yourself down on the list to spend some time alone. You can meditate, talk to yourself, read books that you like, eat food that you love, go shopping for yourself and just focus on You!

Once you start doing this on a regular basis you will notice that you feel much more at peace and less reliant on other people to make you feel important or special, as you will learn that you are special with or without their attention or gifts. You'll soon have the feeling that if they do or don't do, it won't really affect you like it used to since you now are taking care of your own emotions.

It's not about cutting people who are good to you off, it's about allowing those people to not have the added burden of trying to invest more in you than you invest in yourself, and it allows them the extra time that they also need to invest in their own mental wellbeing. Everyone has feelings and needs that only they can fulfill themselves. It all starts with you though. You have to take accountability for yourself and start spending time alone. Get to know who you are.

Fall in love with yourself like never before!

Bonus

A Glance At What Happiness Looks Like

1. You Sleep Better

When I was in toxic relationships in the past with Ex-husbands and with some friends and some family members I hardly ever got a good night's rest. I would toss and turn or wake up in the middle of the night and not be able to go back to sleep because my mind would be wandering and unsettled. I never thought back then that I couldn't sleep well because of the toxic relationships that I had in my life. Years later and after many mental health counseling sessions I discovered that my lack of good rest was directly related to those bad relationships that I had in my life. It's amazing the toll that toxic people can have on your life to the point where you can't even get your proper rest. And when your rest is affected over a period of time it can cause other health problems. But since I've cut all of those people out of my life I sleep like a baby with no cares in the world. Now I feel well rested and calm. And I plan on sleeping well for the rest of my life.

2. Your Energy Increases

Being in bad and unhealthy relationships drains ALL of your energy! Which can make you feel sad and depressed. It also leads to weight gain and a low vibrating mood. When I was in abusive relationships I never felt like doing anything fun most of the time. I would make excuses as to why I didn't want to go to the movies or out for dinner with my friends. Looking back now I can see that it was all because I was feeling sad and I just didn't have the energy to be around other people. Now I go out at least a couple of times a month with friends and just have fun and my energy level is consistently great! I plan and look forward to those fun times! I also take myself out on dates and I enjoy my own company! I even have energy to consistently work out 3 days a week which I never did before.

3. You Feel Calm

Those feelings of anxiety went away once I started loving myself more and getting the mental health therapy that I needed after ending those toxic relationships. Almost instantly I began feeling a sense of self worth which was the initial step to feeling calm. It's like putting the missing pieces to a puzzle in its proper place. Once you identify the problem people in your life, and you stop dealing with them, then you can put yourself back together again. The wholeness that I feel everyday after letting toxic people go, is unspeakable! I feel complete and happy. I feel calm.

4. You Laugh More

Laughter used to be a foreign thing to me because when you're in a toxic relationship there isn't much to even smile about. Everyday it's almost like you're in survival mode. The survival is just to make it through the day without breaking down crying. It's overwhelming when you're unable to think clearly and focus on the daily living activities because your abuser is either making threats to you daily or doing things that make it hard for you to function. Things like having your phone turned off while you're at work because he's mad about something and the phone bill is his name and he wants to be controlling. I'm so thankful to God that I no longer have to deal with anymore manipulation and abuse! I have everything that I need now, and in my own name. I can just breathe and laugh all throughout the day at the silliest things that I never even noticed before. Everyday I laugh several times a day because life is good and I have created an environment filled with gratitude. Laughter is good for the Soul.

5. You Pay More Attention to Your Health

Health is truly Wealth! Oftentimes when we are so focused on everyone else and everything going on around us we will slack off on our own health. From making bad food choices to not getting our check ups when we should to never working out. We forget that we too are important and that our health should actually come first. Because if we are sick then we can't take care of anybody that we care about. One of the first things that I did when I got out of my last abusive marriage was set up an appointment with each Doctor to get a full Physical and Dental and Eye exam. And guess what? I'm in great health Thank God! But I had slacked off for some years on my health check ups and the Doctors told me that if I had waited any longer that I might have been diagnosed with a few different preventable diseases. This would have been all because I didn't take my own health seriously. I thank God that I dodged a bullet so to speak, but now I'm very focused on my health and I make it a priority to stay healthy. I drink water everyday and 90% of what I eat is healthy! I also started working out 3 days a week.

6. You Focus More on Your Purpose and Goals

Now this one is very powerful! You are literally reading this Book as a direct result of me focusing on my purpose after leaving that last toxic marriage!

The moment that I decided that I no longer wanted to be married to a lying, cheating narcissist, was the moment that my mind started refocusing on me and my purpose in life. I have always been a writer and I've always wanted to write this very book. But because of that abusive marriage I could never really put any of my time towards it. But over the course of the past 6 months, I've been able to pull it all together and bring it into fruition! I'm telling you that once you leave any bad relationship, those bad things that came with that person will go away. Then you can begin to put yourself together and start living in your purpose. You can start by writing down your goals and completing them one by one. If I can do it so can You!

7. You Enjoy the Simple Things in Life More

Waking up listening to the birds chirping, or watching the sun rise, or hearing the sound of the ocean water, or even smelling the flowers are things that most of us take for granted on a regular basis. I have recently started taking the time to appreciate the simple things that don't cost us a single penny. The things that are already in place for us to enjoy. You know when you are too busy or preoccupied with this or that, you don't even stop to see the beauty that is all around us. Natural beauty is everywhere. I make it a point now to notice these types of things more than I used to. My mind is clear and free and I can take a few minutes and stand still and give thanks for all of the things that are good in my life. You know it's a blessing within itself to even be able to see and smell. We can all choose to be still sometimes and give thanks and appreciate the simple things in life.

8. You Feel at Peace

The peace that I feel now is indescribable. I will never let go of this feeling of true happiness that I feel inside out. As the saying goes, "once you have peace you don't want to ever lose it".

I pray that you have your peace. ♥

THANK YOU FOR READING MY BOOK!

FREE BONUS GIFT

Just to say thanks for buying and reading my book, I would like to give you a 100% bonus gift for FREE, no strings attached!

To Download Now, Visit:

www.CadoriTheAuthor.com/CM/FreeGift

I appreciate your interest in my book and I value your feedback as it helps me improve future versions of this book. I would appreciate it if you could leave your invaluable review on Amazon.com with your feedback. Thank you!

Made in the USA
Columbia, SC
07 November 2024